RET SELLING

ARBY	BARH	HIST
		5/95
MTRD	CTMOB	GAML
BASS	COMB 6/96	COTT
MELB	SWAV	WILL

RETAIL SELLING

A practical guide for Sales Staff

Len Rogers

KOGAN PAGE

© Len Rogers 1988

All rights reserved. No reproduction, copy or transmission of this publication may be made without written permission.

No paragraph of this publication may be reproduced, copied or transmitted save with written permission or in accordance with the provisions of the Copyright Act 1956 (as amended), or under the terms of any licence permitting limited copying issued by the Copyright Licensing Agency, 7 Ridgmount Street, London WC1E 7AE.

Any person who does any unauthorised act in relation to this publication may be liable to criminal prosecution and civil claims for damages.

First published in 1988 by
Kogan Page Ltd,
120 Pentonville Road, London N1 9JN

Printed and bound in Great Britain by
Billing & Sons Ltd, Worcester

British Library Cataloguing in Publication Data
Rogers, L.A. (Leonard Alfred), *1921-*
   Retail selling: a practical guide for sales staff.
   1. Retailing—Manuals
   I. Title
   658.8'7
   ISBN 1-85091-486-9

Contents

Introduction   9

1. Opening the Sale   13
Knowing and doing. Reason for opening a sale. Don't talk too much. Browsing. Can I help you? Offer products, not help. After the initial greeting.

2. Progressing the Sale   24
After you have opened the sale. I don't know. Objective response. Subjective response. The expert. Unanswerable questions. Value of positive attitude. Use a rifle not a shotgun. Use reasonable questions. Do you want a drink? Greet the customer. Open the sale. Progress the sale.

3. Dealing with Objections   34
When objections arise. Avoid objections. Objections can be disheartening. Can the customer afford it? Types of objections. Decide the type of objection. Objections can be excuses. Real objections. Win an argument and lose a sale. Lessen the impact. Turn the objection into a question. The 'yes, but' technique. The reversal method.

4. Closing the Sale   44
Customers visit you. Concentrate on closing. Make 'em thirsty! The decision to buy. Watch for closing signals. The 'yes' close. Implying that the customer will buy. Assumption by word. Assumption by action. Closing on a minor point. Narrowing the choice. Confusion of choice. The 'last one' close. Closing on an objection. Barrier erecting. Linking with a benefit. Ask for the order. Modifying the product.

5. The Power of Enthusiasm   55
Enthusiasm is persuasive. Don't be a misery. Why people buy. Everyone has problems. Enthusiasm has to be worked at. Secret of enthusiasm. Value of knowledge. Your health. Listen constantly to customers. People are interested in themselves. Knowledge of words. Clichés. Sales sentences. Vocabulary and salary. Practice.
Case Study: The Lightweight Sale
Two sales assistants mishandle a customer who is looking for merchandise and is not satisfied. Readers are invited to consider what went wrong and what should have happened.

6. **Determining the Approach**   65
   The approach. Suspects and prospects. When to approach customers. The best approach. Don't be a highwayman. Don't stand on guard. Knowing your customers. Objectives of a good approach. Eight ways to open the sale. Observation is useful. Three types of customer. Reason for buying. Observe, question and listen. Let the product sell itself. When to comment.

7. **Buying Motives and Selling Points**   75
   Selling points. Unique selling points. Buying points. Buying motives. Selling and buying are the same thing. Customers' backgrounds. Attitudes. Conditions. Physical pleasure. Relaxation and play. Self-esteem and pride. Imitation. Desire to be admired. Our needs. Forget your motives. Where to obtain product information.

8. **Test Closing**   85
   Test continually. If the customer is not ready to buy. Fear of making the wrong purchase. Knowing when to close. Obvious buying signs. A nod of the head. A sparkle in the eye. Tone of the voice. Hesitation. Hesitation and silence. Value of test closing. Closing starts with opening. The customer is likely to buy at any point. Test closing a pen sale. What exactly is the customer buying? Open and closed questions. Open probes. Narrow down or open up conversation.

9. **Working for Repeats**   96
   Customer satisfaction. Frequency of purchase. A customer returns. Type of product and degree of repeat. Enthusiasm stimulates repeat business. Enthusiasm is in oneself. Enthusiasm is infectious. Knowledge plus enthusiasm work for repeats.

10. **Selling Convincingly**   105
    How to avoid scepticism. Bring witnesses to support you. The best witness. Demonstrate products convincingly. Develop dexterity in handling your products. Create confidence with your customer. Stand upright. We are all nervous at times. Eye contact. Speak clearly. No one can communicate. Private languages. Use simple words. Breathe in before you speak. Breathe properly. Most important word. Accents and dialects. 'Um!—er! Well—y' know!' Help the customer to buy. A customer buys a suit. Answers to exercise.
    Case Study: Nelson's Store
    A market survey has been carried out of a menswear store in Bath to establish its image. Readers are invited to consider future sales and merchandising changes and the survey itself.

11. **Sales Policy versus Profit Policy**   118
    Sales policy. Profit. Average stock. Stock-turn. Percentages. Profit is more important than sales. Working all day for your store. Finance to keep a store operating. Work for repeat sales. Customers will like you. Self-service. Comments by customers. A social activity. The telephone. Answering the phone. Be pleased to hear the caller. When you pick up the receiver. Customers can be difficult! Being profit conscious.

12. **Increasing Sales**   128
    Selling more. How to increase your sales. Essential or natural pairing. Complementary not competitive accessories. When to stop?

13. **The Store's Image and Prices**   136
    Creating the image. The intangible image. Image is difficult to change. Selling is a creative activity. Problem of price. When do you mention price? The price bracket. Price is part of the sale. Barrier technique applied to price. The barrier is built. The price image. How to mention price. Defending the price.

14. **Service and Shrinkage**   147
    The concept of service. Before-sales service. During-sales service. Self-service and full service. Shrinkage. Shoplifting. Action to take with a shoplifter. After-sales service. After-sales service not always obvious. Maintaining contact with customers. Small services you can offer.

15. **Making the Most of Your Time**   158
    Time is limited. Maintaining interest. World's most successful company. How to live on 24 hours a day. Knowledge is power. A look at profit. A look at costs. Speed of sales. Percentage on cost and on return. Gross margin and gross profit. Impact of stock. Learn how to handle people. First steps in getting promotion.
    Case Study: Betty Cook's Promotion
    Betty is promoted to assistant buyer and has a number of simple problems. Readers are invited to consider how Betty should approach her new job when her superior, the manager, is away on a course.

16. **How to Improve Continually**   171
    Customers are vital to our business. Increase in self-service. Look efficient—be efficient. Customers come first. Don't judge by appearances. Improving marketing knowledge. The marketing mix. Product. Price. Place. Promotion. Service. Four main forms of service. Service and store image. Routine maintenance. Trading policy.

17. **Buying Motives**   182
    Our real needs. Hierarchy of needs. Selling on the wrong motive. Reasons for buying. Select motive on which to sell. Where the sale takes place. Observe and listen. Susceptibility of customers. Making the right impression. Find out the real reason. Urge to buy a new product. Rationalizing the buying motive. Price as a motive. Why we buy products.

18. **Advertising**   192
    Advertising media. Retail store advertising. Stress what is important. Maintain your image. Offer a promise. Importance of the medium. Appropriate media. Newspaper advertising. Two main advertising situations. Sales literature. Production of adverts and leaflets. Printer's measure. How many words? Outdoor advertising

19. **Getting Results**   **202**
    The losing product. Overheads. Contribution. Previous years.
    Comparing the years. Use of money costs money. Cash flow.

20. **Interpersonal Relationships**   **213**
    Human interactions. The human recording machine. Parent.
    Adult. Child. We three. Normal behaviour. Crossed wires.
    Recognizing parent, adult, child. An apparent paradox. How to
    greet customers. Customers want information. Giving
    information creates confidence. Control the sales presentation.
    Knowledge is the key to control. Out of date knowledge.
    Objections are natural. Objections are not always welcome.
    Objection? Use your adult! Know your product's benefit. Be
    succinct. Put the objection in the sales presentation!
    Case Study: The Grocery Survey
    A survey has been carried out on the grocery shopping habits of a
    sample of people for several supermarkets. Readers are invited to
    assume the role of merchandising manager of one of the stores
    and consider any future changes in merchandising or advertising.

Introduction

Selling concerns everyone

Nearly every day of our life we are involved in one or more retail selling activities. We buy our morning paper, cigarettes, chocolate, petrol, bus or train tickets, morning coffee, sandwiches or lunch, stamps, postcards, personal toiletries—the list is almost endless. These are the products we buy as consumers, mainly for our own use as we need them, on impulse, or when it is convenient. They are called *convenience goods*.

Then there are the goods we tend to buy at weekends—household articles, cutlery, linen, rugs, gardening items, radios, records, cassettes, paint, wallpaper and so on—again, the list is almost inexhaustible. We usually make special shopping trips for these products which are sometimes used or enjoyed by the whole family; they are called *speciality goods*. Before they are purchased, they are often the subject of discussion and a consideration of the merits of competitive offers.

Less frequently, we make major purchases. We buy a car, suite of furniture, bedroom furniture, hi-fi equipment, video-recorder, home computer, a boat and trailer, and similar products which could be classified as consumer capital goods. Their purchase means lengthy assessment and deliberation.

The common denominator

While it is obvious that less selling is involved in the purchase of a packet of chocolate or a bottle of aftershave lotion compared with the acquisition of, say, a new bed, a carpet, or a lawnmower, underlying every retail selling activity is *service*.

The purchaser of the chocolate or aftershave is normally able to select from a variety of products on display and is quickly served by a sales assistant. The purchaser of the bed, carpet, or lawnmower, generally receives extensive information on the manufacture, construction and use of the product. The sales person is able to answer questions and explain points raised by the purchaser. Service is the common denominator.

The essence of selling

No one buys a product for itself alone; only for the satisfaction it provides.

The role of the sales person in retail selling is to communicate those satisfactions, and persuade the customer of the advantages of possessing the product.

Little of this skill is needed when selling convenience goods but, as we move to the more complex speciality products, the role of the retail sales person becomes much more important. If there is one thing, above all others, that an intending purchaser really needs when about to spend a considerable sum of money on a product it is a trained sales person.

A good sales person possesses a fund of knowledge about the products, how they are made, how they are used, what they will do for their owners, and be able to justify the price being asked.

This is no job for amateurs. Retail selling requires trained professionals; people who are prepared to learn about the products they sell, and acquire necessary skills to help customers to make their purchases.

Is this book for you?

If you consider that retail selling is standing in a shop, smiling at customers when they enter, showing them products they ask to see, then taking their money and wrapping up their purchases, this book is *not* for you.

To be a well-trained, effective retail sales person, you need to have a knowledge of:

- Your products and their functions
- How to greet customers and open a sale
- How to show or demonstrate products
- Why people buy

- Dealing with objections
- How to close a sale
- What makes profit
- 'Shrinkage' of stock
- Promotion and advertising
- Personal relationships

If you want to become a professional retail sales person, learn how to use selling skills ethically, and appreciate the wider aspects of retailing, then this book is for you.

You may be in one of the following categories:

- Interested in retail selling and want to make good money
- Some experience of retail selling but wish to improve
- A recent school-leaver interested in retail selling
- In a 'dead-end' job and want to succeed in selling
- Need a change from your present boring job
- A retailer who wishes to increase sales turnover
- Employed in a small retail shop and want promotion
- Unsure about your future but want to 'get into selling'
- Working in a large store and wish to excel in selling
- Own a retail store and wish to develop staff
- Responsible for training retail sales people.

This book will not supply all the answers; for example, it will not give you any information on the products you might be selling, or take you too far into the wider realms of distribution as a whole.

What it will do for you is to show how to sell in a retail outlet, how to progress a sale and cope with the inevitable objections, how to increase sales, how to promote merchandise, how to advertise, how to increase profits. These are some of the things management looks for in staff when promoting them. But, if you are to make a success in retail selling and distribution, you must be able to sell.

You start with an advantage. You don't have to go out and search for customers; they come to you!

A workbook—to help you even more

Just reading about selling is insufficient; you must put it into practice. This is the reason for the *Workbook* that accompanies the main text. It tests your understanding of retail selling skills and how you would apply them in your selling environment. You don't wait until you have read all the book before you start to apply its teaching; you start to implement what you are learning after the first few pages.

Your learning doesn't stop with reading the book: you use the *Workbook* to monitor your progress. You test yourself continuously on what you have read and are practising in your job.

The selling principles that are explained and illustrated with examples in the main text are explored further with various situations, problems and questions in the *Workbook*. You learn how to adapt the principles to real-life situations.

Success in retail selling

If you intend to be successful in retail selling, you need to acquire professional skills that are practical and not academic. Real success in retail selling is possible if you are adequately qualified — qualified to deal with customers, qualified to sell.

Whether you choose to work in a small 'corner shop', a medium size store in the centre of town, or a large multiple retailer, you must specialize in those aspects that suit your own career needs. Successful specialization means developing your knowledge and skills in specific selling directions and not wasting your precious resources learning generalizations.

With *Retail Selling* and its accompanying *Workbook*, you can study at your own pace, adjusting the rate to suit your circumstances.

A *Tutor* for the *Workbook* is available from the publishers.

1
Opening the Sale

Knowing and doing

Knowing what to do and what to say is one thing; actually doing it can be a daunting prospect. When you first start selling, do not be afraid of making mistakes. Always be ready to say, 'I'm sorry', and smile as you say it. It is difficult for a customer to be angry or upset when a sales person says, 'I'm sorry. I didn't realize what you meant. I'll get the right one', or whatever it is, and at the same time smile.

Reason for opening a sale

The only reason you open a sale is because you want to *close it!* Therefore, whenever you open a sale remember that *your aim is to close it.* In retail selling, you close a sale by getting the order. Everything you say and do must have this one end—to close the sale satisfactorily. This must be satisfactory to the customer, satisfactory to you, and satisfactory to the store. Closing sales with customers who are not entirely satisfied is one way to become a very poor sales person.

Salesman:	Good morning, sir, may I help ...	
Customer:	Do you stock Stanley mini-blades?	
Salesman:	Yes, sir, we have	
Customer:	Good! Let me have a dozen, please.	
Salesman:	May I show you ...	
Customer:	No! Just give me a dozen Stanley blades, please.	
Salesman:	But I was going to say	
Customer:	Look, I know what I want. You do stock them, I suppose?	

Salesman: Yes, sir. We have a number of replacement blades in stock. Stanley, Black and Decker, the new Pentel. The new Pentel is very good because...

The salesman looked up from the drawer in which he was searching in time to see the customer disappearing through the door saying that he would call back when he had more time.

Don't talk too much

Don't talk yourself out of a sale. In the Bible we learn that Samson killed ten thousand Philistines with the jawbone of an ass. We wonder how many sales have been killed through the use of too much jawbone!

If the customer knows what he or she needs, there is no point in going through your sales story from the beginning. You must close the sale as quickly as possible—as quickly as the customer wants.

The object of opening a sale is to close it. Therefore, close it as soon as the customer is satisfied that what you are offering is what is needed.

Browsing

You must distinguish between those customers who are just having a look round the shop and those who may be prepared to buy. Do not be disappointed with customers who are not prepared to buy. We all like to spend time browsing in shops. If you approach customers who are just looking round, and your manner is a little too forceful, you can give your store a poor reputation. People will think that they can never walk round the store without being approached. Try to cultivate a 'sense' of the customer who really wants to be served and never use the well-worn question 'Can I help you?'

Can I help you?

This is a very tired and overworked question. It is used mostly to find out whether the customer wants to buy something or is only looking around. If we assume that visitors are going to buy, we run the risk of pestering them. Yet, as a means of ascertaining a customer's intentions—whether to buy or not—asking 'Can I help you?' is almost entirely ineffective. Generally, the answer will be a quick 'no' and you will be further than ever from making a sale.

We must understand why people like to look round a store. Very few people 'just look round' with no possible motive. The majority will become customers in the future, and part of the process of buying a product is to look and ask questions, to compare and assess, to evaluate and decide.

Offer products, not help

Give some though to your particular line of products and you will understand the mechanics of purchasing them. People buy handkerchiefs, for example, when it is convenient. They don't necessarily go from store to store comparing different handkerchiefs and prices.

With products such as washing machines, clothes, carpets, computers and furniture, on the other hand, people do not buy the first they see. They want information and guidance. They look around before they buy. Even if you have a comprehensive selection of makes and models in your store, people like to inspect those in the price range they have in mind. They compare quality, prices, ranges, styles, colours and terms before finally deciding which to purchase. If you sell this type of merchandise, people are going to ask you a lot of questions before they buy. Of course you can help them; that is your job. You do not need to ask them if you can help. Be prepared with product information.

After the initial greeting

Once you have made the initial greeting to a customer and are communicating with him or her, you will know whether or not that customer wishes to be served, to be shown something, or to have further information. You are in a position to open the sale. But before you can do this, you need to have a pretty clear idea of what the customer wants.

At this stage, do not ask, 'May I show you something?' You have to obtain further information from the customer before you

16 RETAIL SELLING

can do this. If you show something at this stage and it is not what is wanted, it could influence the customer against buying.

On the other hand, don't spend minutes questioning the customer before you have something on show. The point is to get a product in front of the customer as quickly as possible but to make sure that you show what you think the customer will buy. Frequently, with good sales people, the first product that is placed before the customer is the one that is eventually purchased, even though several others may have been looked at after the first. Experienced sales people listen carefully to the customer's opening remarks and try to select the right product the first time.

Opening phrases

Compose a number of appropriate opening phrases or short sentences to use in your initial approach to a customer. Here are a few examples of opening greetings:

>Good morning, madam.
>Hello, sir, may I offer you a chair?
>Good afternoon, madam. It's a bit cold outside, isn't it?
>Good afternoon, madam. I hope you find it's nice and cool in here.
>(To customer looking at merchandise) Good morning, madam, that's our new range of ....
>Good afternoon, madam. Perhaps there is something I may show you if it's not on display?
>Good afternoon, sir, is it still raining?

Opening greetings and opening sales

There is a difference between opening greetings and opening the sale. Greeting the customer is the normal 'how do you do?' approach we use in different social and business situations. Opening the sale leads in to the sales presentation.

Importance of listening

Remember what has been said about sales people talking too

much. After you have made your opening greeting, shut up and *listen*.

The customer will probably respond with a similar greeting and then ask to see something, or will ask questions about products, or may even say nothing. In the latter case, you could add, 'Someone is looking after you?' or 'You are being attended to?' It is possible to sell yourself even when it is apparent that the customer is not there to buy at that time.

Salesman:	Good morning, sir.
Customer:	Good morning.
Salesman:	(Pauses) Someone is attending to you, sir?
Customer:	No. I'm waiting for my wife. I don't know what's keeping her. I think she's got lost!
Salesman:	Let me offer you a chair, sir. (Gestures to a chair) Would you like me to try to locate your wife? Is she in another part of the store?

Whatever the customer says at this point, it is possible to help him. If he says that he would welcome your help, then you can take the necessary action. If he says that he is quite prepared to wait, then you could suggest that he browses through your brochures or a newspaper or even looks at your display.

Main opening methods

After the opening greeting has been made, there are different ways in which you can open the sale. The main methods are:

- Introductory opening
- Product opening
- Curiosity opening
- Shock opening
- Statement opening
- Premium opening
- Compliment opening
- Question opening

Introductory opening

The introductory opening is the most widely used. It is also the weakest, because it is not positive, it is over-used and it does not create a dynamic atmosphere. A customer walks into the shop and the salesman says, 'Good morning, madam; may I help you?' or 'Good morning, madam. My name's Brown, how can I be of assistance?' Such approach is pleasant and gains nominal attention, but the addition of the 'may I help you'-type question is not necessary. It is not really the opening of a sale but the extension of the opening greeting.

Product opening

This opening involves actually placing the product in the hands of the customer. If you are selling, say, gloves, or an electric shaver, you might take hold of one glove, or the shaver, and place it in the hands of the customer. This would be pretty silly, of course, if a woman approached you and you shoved a glove into her hand and said nothing. She might respond by saying, 'Thank you, no' or 'Not mine, sorry; where are the toilets, please?'

You must know what the customer is looking for before you can use this opening technique. After the opening greeting, listen carefully to the points made by the customer, weigh them up and then use this opening.

Customer: I'm looking for an electric shaver.
Salesman: Yes, sir. Any particular make?
Customer: Not really. I want to use it when I'm travelling.
Salesman: In this country or abroad as well?
Customer: Hmmm. That's a point. (Pauses, and thinks) Both.
Salesman: (Using product opening, places a model in the customer's hand) That's the one you want. Portable, rechargeable, all voltages; with a very fine, micro-foil head. And very sharp.

If a man comes into your department and looks around, you walk up to him and say 'Good afternoon, sir' and he replies, 'Afternoon. You sell umbrellas?', the product opening might be appropriate. You select a good model and place it in his hand and say nothing, or simply, 'There we are, sir'. It is fairly certain that he will say something, possibly, 'How much?' Notice that we have put the onus on the customer to make a comment.

The product opening should only be used when it is quite natural. Nothing could be more fruitless than if a customer

OPENING THE SALE 19

entered your shop, walked up to you, you both say 'Good afternoon' and then you plonked a single bedspread into her hands! Such an action would qualify more for a comedy sketch than a genuine attempt to sell to a customer.

Curiosity opening

Care must be exercised with this opening; otherwise, you can be too clever. When new product ideas or inventions are highlighted appropriately in the opening, however, the result is both interesting and useful.

>Saleswoman: These two seams hold together, yet there is no visible fastening method.

This approach would be ideal if the customer had asked for a skirt with a hidden zip or if she had expressed any views on conventional fastenings.

A life insurance salesman used to employ a curiosity opening in selling to his clients. He would ask a client 'What would you give me for ten kilos of cork?' to which the customer might reply, 'I don't want any cork', or 'What would I want with ten kilos of cork?' The salesman would respond, 'What would you give me for it if you were in the middle of a lake in a sinking boat?' He would then develop the idea of buying life insurance before the need actually arises.

Always be on the look-out for sales stories from other industries; they can often be adapted to your trade. We might apply this story about the cork to a bedding department. The salesman could say to a prospective customer, 'What do you think three kilos of eiderdown is worth?' After getting the response the salesman could go on to explain that his new duvets contain over three kilos of pure duck down, and to extol his duvets' lightness and heat-retaining virtues.

Thinking about the curiosity opening, this same salesman might pose the question, 'How many miles do you walk in a year just making beds?' He could then develop a sales presentation showing that the use of a duvet dispenses with bed-making.

Shock opening

This is one in which you can confront the customer with some startling fact that she or he might not have known. Consider your range of merchandise carefully and try to present a customer benefit which has a mild element of shock.

A carpet salesman might say to a prospective customer: 'Do you know, sir, a woman wearing high-heeled shoes puts several tons per square inch pressure on a carpet every time she puts her foot down on it? It is advisable to have carpet and underlay that will withstand such pressures.'

You may be selling insurance from a bureau in your store. A suitable opening could be: 'Do you realize the risk you are running when travelling, especially abroad, without adequate medical and other insurance cover?'

Statement opening

The idea behind using this opening is to drive home the advantages of a product fairly quickly. Therefore, simple and direct customer-benefit statements are to be preferred.

> 'You can wash this cardigan in a washing machine as many times as you wish', or 'However many times you wash this, it will not go out of shape'.
> 'No matter how many files and records you have in your company, the whole lot could be stored on these lightweight, laser-read disks.'
> 'These curtains are made from woven glassfibre. They will not burn.'
> 'This is the only bedspread we sell. It's the finest we can buy at the price and our experience is to sell only this one. None of the others can compare with it in value, quality and wear.'
> 'You can buy a similar item about two-thirds our price but we know from our customers' reports that our product will last more than twice as long.'
> 'Even if you dropped this from a high building on to concrete it would not break and you would not damage the mechanism.'

Use simple, direct, truthful statements relating to customer-benefits.

Premium opening

This opening rests on the human urge to get something for nothing, and puts the customer in a positive frame of mind toward the product.

A manufacturer of skirts might offer a handbag-sized brush with his name printed on the brush. A manufacturer of tape recorders offers a magnetic tape-head cleaning tape. A furniture retailer offers a stool with every suite sold. An electricity showroom offers a 'free' electric iron to every person buying a washing machine. A bedding manufacturer might offer a perpetual calendar with washing and dry-cleaning hints on the reverse. A motor car dealer offers a week's holiday abroad to every buyer of a certain car.

Such premiums are offered quite freely to prospective customers when they visit the retail outlet. These special offers are forms of advertising that are usually promoted by the manufacturers.

Compliment opening

Take care with this opening because it can sound patronizing. 'That's a beautiful colour, madam.' She may hate it!

It is better to personalize your compliments by saying 'Madam, I *do* like that colour'. The secret of giving a genuine compliment is sincerity. Be sincere, be honest and do not be afraid of your compliment. On the other hand, be careful not to overstep the mark and be too effusive. The compliment would sound hollow and you would sound insincere. A little flattery, lightly used, is like seasoning used in cooking—complementary and not overpowering. Jonathan Swift wrote:

> 'Tis an old maxim in the schools
> That flattery's the food of fools
> Yet, now and then, your man of wit
> Will condescend to take a bit.

Question opening

This is the most fruitful opening for a sales presentation, but great care should be taken in constructing the question. You should write possible questions down on paper and try them on your colleagues before you use them in actual situations.

The reason for opening a sale with a question is to get the customer involved. You want to get the customer to say, 'May I see it?' or some similar expression of interest.

Consider the situation of a store buyer confronted with a salesman who has good products to sell. The buyer does not know the salesman or his company.

Salesman: Do you have the kind of outlet that could sell high grade products?

There are very few answers to that opening question that would put the salesman on the defensive. In most instances, the buyer would be on the defensive. His or her replies would fall into two main categories — those that indicate that the buyer does not have a high grade outlet (this reply is highly unlikely) and those which stress that the buyer is already selling high grade products. Here are some of the possible answers:

Salesman: Do you have the kind of outlet that could sell high grade products?
Buyer: We're selling them now...
Salesman: I'm sorry. I didn't make myself quite clear about the kind of products I mean.
Buyer: What kind do you mean?

Now the salesman can go into his sales presentation and explain what it is he is selling.

Salesman: Do you have the kind of outlet that could sell high grade products?
Buyer: We have the best products on the market now, thank you.
Salesman: I'm talking about a different kind of product.
Buyer: What kind of product are you talking about?

And so into the sales presentation.

Salesman: Do you have the kind of outlet that could sell high grade products?
Buyer: We're quite satisfied with the range we are selling now.

Salesman:	But couldn't your shop sell a high grade product?
Buyer:	What kind of product do you mean?

Again, the salesman can go into his presentation.

You can see how a carefully phrased question that gets attention, yet does not give offence, can be used to get a prospective buyer to see what is being offered.

If it is appropriate, when next a woman customer asks to see some summer dresses, why not try, 'Would you like to see some patterned prints that are selling in Paris (or wherever) now?' It would be difficult to imagine a customer saying 'no, thank you' but even if she did, you would have at least progressed the sale to the next stage.

Also, if appropriate, if a man walks into your shop and says he would like to see what electronic typewriters you have, you could say 'Would you like to see the latest generation of word processors that have revolutionized the electronic officel' It is a fairly easy way to pass to the next stage.

2
Progressing the Sale

After you have opened the sale

After you have opened the sales presentation, you have to progress it logically towards a satisfactory close. Saying 'good morning', or whatever, to a customer is not opening a sale: it is merely establishing contact. As soon as you have greeted the customer, you must decide whether or not to start the selling presentation. Once you have opened the sale, you must progress it carefully towards a close.

The greatest help to opening and progressing a sale is to observe and listen. You can understand a lot by observing people: what they are wearing, how they conduct themselves, whether they are positive and know what they want or whether they are undecided. Listen carefully to everything that is said, however insignificant, because *listening is probably your greatest ally in selling*.

Consider the following:

Customer:	Good morning.
Saleswoman:	Good morning, madam.
Customer:	I'm looking for a lightweight dress. Something really lightweight.
Saleswoman:	Certainly, madam. Any particular colour?
Customer:	Well, I don't like green.
Saleswoman:	Would this be for formal wear?
Customer:	Well—er—um...
Saleswoman:	May I ask, when will you be wearing it?
Customer:	Well, generally, but—er—what type of dress do you think would be best for a garden party?
Saleswoman:	It depends whether it's a formal affair where you would need to have hat and gloves, or just an informal party.

PROGRESSING THE SALE 25

As you can see, the sale is being progressed.

Salesman: Good morning, sir.
Customer: Good morning. I'm looking for a lampshade.
Salesman: For a standard lamp, or ceiling?
Customer: Ah! Standard lamp.
Salesman: Any preference for material? Silk? Synthetic?
Customer: I'm not sure. Can I have a look at something?
Salesman: Certainly. We have many on display, as you can see. Which room is it for, sir?
Customer: Sitting room.
Salesman: Is there a general colour scheme or do you have a particular colour in mind?
Customer: Well, not blue.
Salesman: And do you use this lamp for reading or close work, or is it for background light?

Another situation:

Salesman: Good afternoon, sir.
Customer: Afternoon. (Approaches a display of products and walks round it, stopping occasionally, and examining goods on display) I see you've got one or two different mixers here. What's the main difference between them?
Salesman: Mainly power, size and variable speed.
Customer: I just want a simple one. No gadgets.
Salesman: Well, this is the lowest price mixer. It's hand-held, fixed speed, and useful for all types of mixing.
Customer: What about drinks?
Salesman: Ideal. Do you want it only for drinks?
Customer: No, but that's a main reason. What's the advantage of a variable speed mixer?
Salesman: Versatility mainly. You have the right speed for the particular application. With a fixed speed mixer, there's a compromise between the various possible uses. So things that normally need a high speed mix, you have to do a little longer. With variable speed you can mix drinks at low speed and, say, mayonnaise, at a very high speed.
Customer: What's the difference in price?

Salesman:	Of which, sir? (Examining the products) These two?
Customer:	Yes.
Salesman:	£5. The variable mixer is £5 more than the fixed speed. But, in addition to the variable speed control, you get different mixing heads, an eggwhite separator and a rack to hold it all.

And so on. These are all typical situations: the sales person progresses the sale by asking questions to find out what the customer really needs.

I don't know

Frequently, you will be in a position where the customer wants to make a purchase but is not sure which product to choose. Often, you will be asked for your opinion: 'Which do you think?'

You must be careful how you deal with this question. If you are considerably younger than the customer, you will probably be at a disadvantage unless you can demonstrate that you are a real professional and know the products thoroughly. If you are much older than the customer, you could be at an advantage; you might also be at a disadvantage because you are not 'with it'!

You can see how important it is to observe and listen.

Never answer the question 'Which do you think?' unless you are sure of your answer. The question might be about the correct form of dress, the correct type of electrical apparatus, the best adaptable equipment or the most suitable machine, or it might simply have to do with personal preference.

Objective response

The customer's question, 'Which do you think?', relates to either an objective or subjective point. If it is a question of which model or product is the more appropriate or correct for the customer's operation, the answer must be objective.

Customer:	Which do you think?
Salesman:	It has to be this one, sir. With that one, you're restricted to only two external points and you said you need three, so this is the one you need.

PROGRESSING THE SALE

Customer: Ah! Yes!

The response has to be objective.

Customer: Which do you think?
Saleswoman: I think it's got to be this one, madam. It's a hundred per cent drip-dry, non-iron and, as you will be travelling, you won't always have the facilities for washing and ironing, and hotel laundering isn't always the answer. I know the others are recommended for travelling but they won't stay as nice as this one.
Customer: Hmm!

Again, the response has to be objective.

Subjective response

If the question relates to personal preference, perhaps of colour, weight or performance, then the customer is really asking for your help in making a decision to buy. This could be looking for support for his/her own unspoken, or subconscious, preference.

Customer: Which do you think? The blue or the turquoise?
Customer: Which do you think is the best? This one with ten memories and full wave band spread, or this one with two more memories but a little less on the short wave spread?
Customer: Which do you think? They're both variable speed but should it be the ABC or the XYZ?

These questions require subjective responses. Whenever you are in doubt as to the correct information, ask a senior colleague.

You are not belittling yourself to the customer by saying 'I'll just ask Miss Smith because she is an authority on that'.

The fact that you can speak in such a confident matter will convince the customer that here is a sales person who knows where and how to get expert advice.

The expert

The expert is not the person who knows everything, but the

person who knows where to go for the answers! Thus, by knowing your products and the people who have experience in their application and use, you can very easily become an expert. You will know how to get the answers.

If you attempt to give advice to a customer on the purpose of an article — the right dress to wear at a formal garden party; whether a hat should be worn at a school 'open' day; if cellular wool blankets are all right to use with nylon sheets; whether lace curtains can be 'ruffled'; whether a piece of electrical equipment will connect with a customer's present equipment; if one computer program is compatible with other equipment; can it be used on the US electrical system, and so on — and you do not really know the answers, your attempt to 'help' the customer will fail. And so will any confidence between you.

The customer may find out that he knows more about it than you do, and then you have lost control of the sale. Always take advice but do so by saying 'I will ask so-and-so, who knows about these things', and do not say, 'I don't know'. You will not always know the answers, but you must know where to get them.

Unanswerable questions

The day when there are no questions that can be asked of you that you cannot answer, will be the day when you have ceased to work! Every day of your life you are likely to be asked questions with which you are completely unable to cope. But don't say 'I don't know', and never say 'I haven't the faintest idea'. Think about that for a moment. Someone asks 'What's the time?' How often do we hear the reply 'Haven't the faintest idea'. The fact is that we always have a fairly good idea of the time and it is possible to make a reasonable estimate. Test this the next time someone asks you this very question. Estimate the time without looking at your watch: you will surprise yourself how near you can be to the actual time.

When a customer approaches you and asks you a question which you think you can't answer, it is unnecessary to say 'I don't know'. It lays the wrong foundation; it implies that you are unwilling to go further. You are not really interested in the customer's problem and you are not going to develop the sales presentation.

How can we reconcile the comments made in this chapter — that we should always be ready to consult an expert rather than answer

PROGRESSING THE SALE

when we are not sure—and, on the other hand, that we should be willing to make an estimate?

Value of positive attitude

The answer is that both show a positive attitude. To say 'I don't know' is a negative statement. To say 'I'll ask Mr Goodman who is an authority on that' or 'I am not sure but I'll ask Mr Goodman because he is an authority on that' is a positive approach. You progress sales by taking positive attitudes to customers' problems and making positive statements. These lead to the closing of the sale.

Positive action is making sure that the customer knows the benefits of the particular merchandise you are selling at that time.

Remember that no one buys a product for itself alone but for the service or satisfaction it gives.

Therefore make positive statements about your products that suggest specific customer benefits: specific customer benefits rather than general customer benefits because you must find out what a customer needs.

Use a rifle, not a shotgun

If your aim is good, the rifle sends one bullet directly to the centre of the target; a shotgun sprays shot in profusion all round it. The best way to determine a customer's specific needs is to ask questions, but not in a manner that subjects the customer to the 'third degree'!

Customer: Good morning.
Salesman: Good morning, sir.
Customer: I'm interested in buying a video-recorder.
Salesman: Ah! You couldn't have come at a better time. We have a couple of special offers at the moment. One with remote-control, the other manual. Would you want remote-control?
Customer: Well...
Salesman: And, I daresay, you'd like at least three recording blocks. I take it you're not interested in stereo are you? By the way, are you familiar with VCR operation, sir? Here are

the two models on special offer, both connected to TVs as you can see there. What do you think?

The shotgun has peppered this customer with questions and left little room for replies.

Customer: Good afternoon. I'd like to see some curtaining material please.
Salesman: Certainly, madam. What colour? Would this be for the kitchen, the bedroom or the sitting room?
Customer: Well, I think...
Salesman: Any particular material you have in mind? We have some beautiful lace just in from Belgium. What colour did you say?
Customer: I'm not sure. I'd like to know...
Salesman: Oh! We have some remnants here. How many yards do you need?
Customer: About—er—I didn't measure—er...
Salesman: Would you like to see some velvets?
Customer: No.
Salesman: What about a flower print?
Customer: I don't think so. But...
Salesman: Would you like us to make them up for you?

The customer doesn't stand a chance! In fact, neither does the salesman—if making a good sale is his aim.

The secret of progressing the sale is to listen to the customer's statements and his or her responses to your suggestions and questions. Deal with each point, one at a time. Give the customer time to respond. You know the product; if you are selling it every day, you will know the product 'backwards'. It may be the first time that the customer has looked at it. Progress the sale by listening to what the customer says; develop your presentation by making use of those responses.

Use reasonable questions

When you ask questions, make the reasons for your questions perfectly clear to the customer but avoid appearing rude.

Salesman: Good morning.

PROGRESSING THE SALE

    Customer: Good morning. I would like some swimwear, please.
    Salesman: Are you going on holiday?

Although the question is clear, it is too blunt.

    Salesman: Good morning.
    Customer: Good morning. I would like some swimwear, please.
    Salesman: Certainly. Suitable for beach wear?

The salesman asks a question to help him progress the sale by selecting the swimwear most suitable. He will need to explore further before narrowing down to the type of swimwear appropriate for the customer. For example, he doesn't know whether it is for the customer or is being bought for someone else.

    Salesman: Good afternoon, sir.
    Customer: Good afternoon. I want a very lightweight suit, please. Do you stock them?
    Salesman: Yes, sir. Are you going abroad?

Not a very good question. Too intrusive. The following would be better:

    Salesman: Yes, sir. Would this be for tropical wear, holiday wear, or for more formal business occasions?

Where possible, make questions specific and suggest ideas and uses at the same time.

    Customer: Good afternoon. I'd like to see a photostat machine, please.
    Salesman: What kind do you have in mind?

This is playing ping-pong with words without progressing the sale. Make a suggestion, or ask a question that enables you to see the customer's problem.

    Salesman: How many copies are you considering each week? A dozen or so, or are we in the hundreds?

    Customer: I'd like to some single bedspreads, please.
    Saleswoman: Certainly, madam. What kind are you looking for?

Ping-pong again. Make a suggestion.

Saleswoman: Would you like a heavy-weight, loose drape style or a lightweight one with a semi-fitted cover?

The customer may say that neither is wanted but at least you are progressing the sale.

Saleswoman: What colour do you prefer?

This is seldom a good way to develop the sale. You should make a suggestion that is reasonable.

Saleswoman: Do you prefer a pale shade or a stronger colour?

Do you want a drink?

The next time you are being entertained socially, especially in a more formal occasion, rather than with friends who are likely to ask, 'What are you having?', listen to the way you are invited to have a drink. How much nicer it is for someone to ask you 'What would you like: a sherry, whisky, gin and tonic, or perhaps a campari and soda?' This is much better than 'Would you like a drink?', or even worse, 'Do you want a drink?'

Employ this same technique when you are asking customers questions. Offer them a choice, a positive choice, and you will progress the sale more quickly.

To summarize what we have looked at so far:

Greet the customer

Acknowledge the presence of a customer. Don't wait for the customer to walk up to you before you say good morning or whatever it is. Walk towards the customer and say good morning or good afternoon. Smile! You are pleased to see the customer; that is why you are there. If you have no customers, soon you will have no job! If you are doing something when a customer approaches, leave it and carry on when the customer has left. If you happen to be talking to another shop employee, stop immediately and pay attention to the customer. This should be done even if you are talking with the shop manager or owner.

Open the sale

Make use of the various ways of opening the sale, but do not try to use them all. Concentrate on developing your own personal way of opening. Distinguish between opening the sale and continuing the initial greeting. Avoid falling back on the hackneyed question 'Can I help you?'

Selling in a retail outlet has a special advantage for you: the customer has called on you and has to make the first move. Listen carefully to what is said and then use your opening accordingly. Remember that you open a sale to close it!

Progress the sale

Progress the sale by helping the customer to buy. Explore the customer's needs with questions, but ask them in the right way. Don't interrogate the customer. With pleasant, helpful enquiries, find out what the customer really needs. When you think that you have discovered what will satisfy the customer, talk about product benefits and link these with the customer needs. Be positive, not negative. Instead of saying 'I don't know' say 'I know someone who knows'.

3
Dealing with Objections

When objections arise

Objections will usually arise during a sales presentation. Sometimes they are minor and sometimes they are fundamental. You must learn to expect them and deal with them accordingly. You are not trying to win a game with a customer. But at the same time, you must learn to identify the different types of objections you will meet.

Avoid objections

Undoubtedly the best way of dealing with objections is to avoid them. But this is not possible all the time. It helps, however, if you recognize that behind every customer's objection, sincere or not, is fear. Fear that he or she is making a mistake. Fear of the consequences of a wrong decision. Fear of spending too much; buying the wrong colour; buying the wrong product; buying at the wrong time, and so on. Your job is to find out what exactly the customer is afraid of.

Objections are part of the selling process and must be expected as a normal function of the sale. If you can anticipate them and lessen their impact, then you will be a better sales person. 'To anticipate' means to take action before an expected event. Prepare yourself to deal with objections by taking the appropriate action before they arise. This means knowing as much as possible about your products, how they are used and what they will do for a customer.

DEALING WITH OBJECTIONS 35

Objections can be disheartening

You will probably feel a little disheartened when you first hear objections raised by customers, especially when you are first attempting to sell. But don't be. Objections are natural and can assist you by indicating how far you are from closing the sale. Sincere objections can be an expression of sincere interest, so you must find out if the objection is sincere or just an excuse for not buying at the moment.

Can the customer afford it?

A customer may be impressed by your presentation and really want to buy the product but does not have the ready money at that time. In this situation, a customer sometimes raises any objection other than the real one—lack of money. Obviously, if you realized that lack of money was the real reason, you would be foolish to press the matter.

Most stores have a scheme for spreading payments over a period, sometimes with little or no charge for the extended credit. Introduce the point pleasantly and obliquely.

Customer: Hmm! I like it—but...
Saleswoman: Yes, it suits you very well.
Customer: Yes. It's quite expensive, though.
Saleswoman: Well, for the quality, the price is very reasonable.
Customer: (Hesitating) Hmm! I think I'll leave it for the moment.
Saleswoman: You can take advantage of our extended credit terms, of course, if you like.

This won't do at all. It's too brusque and the saleswoman has not found out whether lack of funds is the reason for not closing. This is better:

Customer: Yes. It's quite expensive, though.
Saleswoman: Well, for the quality, the price is very reasonable.
Customer: (Hesitating) I think I'll leave it for the moment.
Saleswoman: Certainly, madam. But you wouldn't want to go for a lower quality, would you?

Customer: Oh! No.
Saleswoman: Apart from the price, you think it's ideal?
Customer: Yes. Indeed.
Saleswoman: Why don't you take advantage of our interest-free scheme? You pay the same price but over six months.
Customer: I don't think so, thank you.
Saleswoman: Lots of our regular customers do. It means that they have the use of their money to earn interest as well as not having to pay the store interest. There are no formalities. It's not like hire purchase. It's simply a service we provide for our regular customers.

If you have made your presentation properly, and the product is what the customer really wants, sooner or later the purchase will be made.

Types of objections

Objections may be classified as: imagined objections; excuses or pretend objections; and real objections. In addition, in logical terms, an objection may be valid or invalid. If valid, the objection is justifiable and can be proven; if invalid, the objection does not accord with the facts. Do not confuse this with an objection being true or untrue.

Validity follows from logical argument. For example: all Frenchmen are Europeans; this man is a Frenchman; therefore this man is a European. This is a valid argument.

But consider the same pattern of argument. All Frenchmen are Americans; this man is a Frenchman; therefore this man is an American. The argument is valid in terms of logic, but it is not true, because the premise of the argument is false.

Sometimes you will hear a valid objection which, in fact, is not true. The customer may be imagining things about the product. Alternatively, the customer may be pretending or raising a sincere, real objection. You can't win arguments with customers and therefore you must listen, learn and, with experience, decide how to deal with the objection.

Decide the type of objection

You have to decide which of the three the customer is using. Obviously, you can't ask the customer what kind of objection is being used but, if you develop your sales technique by helping the customer to buy, you will often be able to detect the type of objection being raised.

Salesman: I think that covers the general description of the product.
Customer: Yes, but there's no way to adjust the output. It's no good if I can't adjust the output.
Salesman: (Knows this is an invalid objection and imagined by the customer) Agreed, sir. Output has to be maintained according to the power input. Right?
Customer: Of course! That's what it's all about.
Salesman: With this product, it's done for you automatically. You see this indicator light here? (Points) It stays lit to tell you that output is being monitored and automatically adjusted. In fact, this is done every half second. That's a little faster than it can be done manually!
Customer: Hm!

The objection raised by the customer may be valid, but the disadvantage is only imagined. The customer has to be helped.

Salesman: That covers the general description, I think. Anything specific you'd like to ask?
Customer: No. I think it's fine. It will do all that I want. However, it's a little too heavy, I think. I wouldn't want one that heavy.
Salesman: (Knows that the objection is valid but imagined) Now you did say you had to have automatic monitoring?
Customer: Yes. That's essential. Well, not essential, but that's what I want in the new one.
Salesman: Right. And you said the take-up and ejection must also be automatic? Not essential, but that's what you want.
Customer: Yep!

Salesman:	Those two facilities account for the extra weight. Have you any idea of the difference in weight between what you are using now and this one?
Customer:	Not really.
Salesman:	If you'll open your hand and shut your eyes, I'll place in your palm something that equals the extra weight. (Does so)
Customer:	(Opening his eyes) Good gracious. Is that all?
Salesman:	Yes. The difference is just 50 grams. It is heavier. You're right, but the reason you think it's much heavier is not so much the weight, it's the different shape to what you have been used to.
Customer:	Hm!

To be able to deal with objections, you must know your products thoroughly. Try not to be in the position in which the customer knows more than you about your products. Of course, this will happen, but, in general, you should be the expert.

Objections can be excuses

If the objection is simply an excuse for not buying, despite the fact that you have the impression that the customer wishes to have the product, then you must try to answer the objection so that the customer is led to the close. Such objections are not real, but part of the natural defensive mechanism of customers. However, it takes time and experience to deal with this difficult type of objection. You can't argue with the customer; you can't say that the customer is just making excuses.

The best way of dealing with an objection that you think is an excuse is to treat it as a real objection.

Customer:	No! I'm sorry, but I don't think I'll take it today.
Salesman:	You'd like to leave it for now?
Customer:	Yes, please.
Salesman:	I can easily put it on one side for you. Would you like me to do that?
Customer:	No. I don't think so.
Salesman:	It's no trouble I assure you.

DEALING WITH OBJECTIONS 39

Customer: Yes, but the...

...and often the real reason comes out. The salesman has treated the objection for what it is. A pretend objection. The customer has used it to screen the real reason.

Real objections

Genuine objections are sometimes raised by customers after a thoughtful consideration of the sales person's presentation and an inspection of the product. These objections are not excuses. If they represent obstacles that you can overcome, your course is clear. But you must take the customer's objections seriously, and to deal with them you must know your product thoroughly.

As soon as you hear a real objection, restate it in your own words so that the customer knows that you understand it. This builds confidence between you, and lays the groundwork for future sales.

If you know how to solve the problem identified by the customer, you can still make the sale. Restate the objection in your own words. Stress that if the offending disadvantage were not present, or could be overcome, the product would be satisfactory. When the customer has agreed, show how the objection can be overcome.

Remember, however, that you are not trying to win an argument. You are helping the customer to buy. The objection is as much a problem for you to overcome as it is for the customer. Therefore, treat all objections with respect and sincerity. Make sure the customer knows that you understand the objection, then remove the basis for it.

Win an argument and lose a sale

Even when you know that the customer is making a mistake, do not correct the error. Appear to agree but add that, in certain instances, such as the one in which you are now engaged, the opposite view could be taken. If a customer makes a statement that is not correct, and it doesn't really matter as far as the sale is concerned, there is not the slightest advantage in correcting it.

Suppose you had a customer who was trying on various gloves and you didn't possess the size that the customer wanted in the material required. If that customer made an objection about the

40   RETAIL SELLING

gloves that was incorrect, there'd be no sense in correcting that statement. You don't have the gloves in the size anyway. You could win the argument and probably damn a sale for all time.

Customer:	As far as I can see, you don't have any size six and a half in this unlined cape.
Saleswoman:	I'm sorry, no.
Customer:	In any case, they're all very much too expensive.

You may know your merchandise very well and know that your price for these gloves is keener than anywhere else. But you can see how needless it is to argue with the customer and 'win' the argument. The overriding strategy must be never to argue with customers. Let us look at some techniques for dealing with objections.

Lessen the impact

Lessen the impact of the objection by listening. Never interrupt a customer who is stating an objection. This is a lot more difficult than it sounds. What you have to do is to listen without saying anything until the customer has finished making the objection.

Imagine that the objection is like a blown-up balloon that is slowly, or rapidly, having its air let out. When the customer has finished making the objection, restate the objection in simple terms but do not exaggerate or magnify it. Objections are frequently made in emotional language and often with some slight emotion on the part of the customer. If you listen to the objection and then restate it in simple, unemotional terms, it often becomes clear just how minor the objection really is.

Customer:	No, thank you. I don't think I'll buy it. Pullovers like this always shrink. After washing they go out of shape. I like it but it's too expensive for what it is. (Pauses) I had one similar to this last year. I just don't like this material. Nothing looks worse than a pullover that gets out of shape. (Long pause)
Saleswoman:	I agree. Pullovers that shrink or go out of shape are expensive at any price. Fortunately, this make is guaranteed to

DEALING WITH OBJECTIONS 41

keep its shape and not to shrink even if it is washed in a machine. It's entirely new.

Lessen the objection by listening. If you attempt to interrupt a customer during an objection you will soon be arguing with that customer.

Turn the objection into a question

By turning the objection into a question you can often change it into a question that you can answer.

Customer: I like the look of this cardigan but, dear me, the pockets are much too small. You see, I want it for when I'm teaching. The pockets really are much too small.

Saleswoman: That's a good point, madam: Are the pockets large enough to hold a multitude of things when you are teaching? How many things would you want to put in your pocket by the way?

Customer: Well—er—certainly not the blackboard rubber but a—er—but supposing I did!

Saleswoman: Let's look at this little box here. Would this be as big as a blackboard rubber?

Customer: Much bigger, in fact.

Saleswoman: Well, we'll put this in one of the pockets. See? Here are also a couple of pencils, a notebook, my diary... See how the elastic nature of the fabric permits it to stretch to nearly four times its size? A lot of customers are amazed with this fabric. It will not go out of shape and will always spring back to its original shape!

Learn to turn objections into questions. Of course, this only works if you can answer the question! But if you can handle objections in this way, you need no longer be in the difficult position of trying to prove that you are right. All you need to do is to answer the question you put to the customer.

The 'yes, but' technique

Here, you agree with the objection and then point out some other feature or take the objection and pull it apart. When selling some curtain material, a salesman met the following objection with the 'yes, but' method.

>Customer: I like the pattern but such a strong blue will fade in the sun.
>Salesman: Yes, it will. In fact, all colours fade eventually; some more quickly than others.

The salesman agrees with the customer and then adds a 'but'. He did not actually say 'but'; he said, 'in fact'. While this is called the 'yes, but' method, you should try not to use these actual words because they are overworked and have negative ideas attached to them. It is better to use phrases which mean much the same thing yet which are softer. The word 'unless' is a good word to use.

>Customer: I don't want to pay that much.
>Salesman: Neither would I, sir... unless I knew I were getting extra value for the outlay, as you would be in this case.

Other words you can use are: 'although' and 'on the other hand'.

The reversal method

A useful technique for the more experienced sales person is the reversal method which takes the objection and uses it as the reason why a prospective customer should buy.

>Customer: I don't think I'll buy that branded product. They spend so much on advertising it's bound to be too dear.
>Salesman: Madam, that's one of the strongest reasons for having it. This company has such a wonderful reputation to maintain they really do have to put the finest value into their product.

To summarize on dealing with objections:

- Lessen the impact of the objection by listening.

DEALING WITH OBJECTIONS 43

- Convert the objection into a question and then answer the question.
- Use the 'yes, but' method of agreeing but indirectly deny the objection because of another benefit.
- Use the reversal method, sometimes called the boomerang method because it uses the objection as a reason for buying.
- Always remember the underlying strategy: never argue with customers.

4
Closing the Sale

Customers visit you

Your job is made easier by the fact that people visit you. They expect to buy something sooner or later. You are not in the same position as a sales person calling on your company trying to sell something. The majority of your customers visit the store with the intention of buying. Therefore, you must expect to close sales; it is normal for you to do so.

Concentrate on closing

A good sales person is always a good closer. A poor sale closer is always a poor sales person. Everything that you have done up to the point of closing has but one objective—to make a sale.

Imagine the kind of success a football team would have if it played excellent football, was able to pass the ball backwards and forwards and from side to side, had superior men who could beat the opponents, but never scored any goals!

Make 'em thirsty

There is an apt story about a salesman who was complaining to his manager about his inability to get prospective customers to close.

    Salesman: I can lead them right up to the water, but I can't make them drink.
    Manager: Your job is not to make them drink but to make 'em thirsty!

Here is one of the successful ideas behind successful closing. You must make your customers want the goods you are showing them more than they want the money that the goods cost. A sale is made in the mind of the buyer and successful closing is to 'make the customer thirsty'!

The decision to buy

To understand how people decide on buying an article, think of the last time you went out shopping to buy something that cost a substantial amount of money. Doubtless, you had a good look round to see what was available and then, gradually, became 'thirsty' for one particular product. At some particular point you *decided to buy* and the sale was 'closed'. This is often called the 'psychological moment' — the right time to close — but it is very difficult to pinpoint because you cannot see into the customer's mind.

Some customers signal this moment by shrugging their shoulders, sighing, holding their breath, touching their face with their hands, leaning forwards, leaning backwards, and so on. There is really no limit to the number of different signals. If you could detect that so-called psychological moment you would make many more sales because, all too often, we talk ourselves beyond that point. In other words, we talk ourselves out of a sale.

Watch for closing signals

Watch customers closely to see if you can detect a pattern of behaviour at the moment when they have decided to buy.

There are a number of ways to close a sale. You may use any one or more of them in attempting to close depending on the particular difficulties or circumstances you meet. They can also be used in combinations. Work out your own variations of them and remember, you can't sell if you can't *close*!

The 'yes' close

This method of closing means that you construct questions to the customer all the way through your sales presentation to obtain 'yes' responses. By doing this, the customer becomes so accustomed to saying 'yes' that, by the time the close is attempted, the customer will say 'yes' from habit.

46   RETAIL SELLING

The reasoning behind this is that if the sales person puts a series of questions that allow the customer to admit that he or she wants the benefit of possession of the product, then, when the sales person goes for the close, the customer will admit wanting to possess the product itself.

Salesman: You will appreciate that this is a very powerful and versatile chess computer.
Customer: Yes. I can see that.
Salesman: You would find it very useful when travelling.

Note here the use of the word 'would' rather than 'will' because the salesman is not quite sure at this point whether the customer is going to buy. If he had used the word 'will', he would be test, or trial, closing. More of this later.

Customer: Yes, and at home of course.
Salesman: You can operate it silently by switching off the bleep signalling that it's your turn to play and, if you don't notice that it's moved, you can look back to review the moves. You can actually look back up to six moves so it's fine for game analysis.
Customer: Yes, I think it's excellent.
Salesman: You have a car? (Notices the customer's car keys)
Customer: Yes.
Salesman: Well, one of the advantages of this set is that you can run it from the cigar lighter in the car as well as from the AC mains adaptor and, of course, from its own batteries. They give about 24 hours of continuous play. You would find it a very versatile set.
Customer: Yes, indeed.

The salesman has obtained a continuous affirmation of the customer benefits without appearing to sound artificial. Soon the customer will want to affirm his desire to possess the electronic chess set.

Implying that the customer will buy

This is where you assume, by word or action, that the prospect has made up his or her mind to buy. The value of this approach is that if the prospective customer does not stop you, you can conclude that everything is all right and go for a close.

Never be afraid of assuming that the customer intends to buy. You have not made a special journey to seek out the customer; the customer has come to see you. It is perfectly natural to assume that the customer intends to buy.

Assumption by word

> Salesman: As you are laying this stair carpet yourself, you would prefer to have it delivered towards the end of the week, I presume. This will give you the weekend to put it down.

Note the use of the word 'will' in the final sentence.

> Salesman: You thought beige would be better, didn't you, madam? You're right. It would be better as it will not show dog hairs. And it will be very easy to keep looking nice. It will be the beige, then?

The word 'will' is used again. Also notice the word 'nice'. If your customer is one who would tend to use words other than the overworked 'nice', you should consider using 'elegant', 'admirable', 'distinctive', 'magnificent', 'incomparable', 'imposing' or 'impressive'. The question, 'It will be the beige, then?' is only partly a question. It is really a statement worded like a question but spoken in such a way as to gain the customer's assent. To achieve this, your voice should drop down at the end rather than be raised in the form of a question.

If your customer is not to be rushed, instead of saying, 'It will be the beige, then', say 'Assuming you take the beige, then' or 'If you take the beige, then', because occasionally a customer will not close if it appears that there is an attempt to rush the sale.

Assumption by action

You may give the impression that the sale has been closed if you clear a space on the counter, fetch wrapping paper or a bag, open your cash sales book, or partly fold, close or replace the article in its box in front of the customer. These are physical acts that assume that the sale has been concluded.

Closing on a minor point

It is easier for people to make a minor than a major decision. Therefore, you can make it easier for your customers to buy if you avoid their having to take the decision, 'Yes, I will buy', and you substitute a minor one which they will find easier to take. A carpet salesman might say to a customer, 'I know you'd like to have one of these. Should we send the one with the plain ends or the other?' or 'Do you wish to pay now or take advantage of our extended credit scheme—it will cost you no more?' The secret of this form of closing is not to ask 'if', but 'which'.

Narrowing the choice

This close is useful in those situations in which the customer has so many possible choices that it is difficult to decide. Here you should try to narrow down the choice to not more than two or three.

In the 'A' situation, the customer has two choices and is undecided as to which. You can frequently progress this situation and get a decision by introducing a third possibility. This third offer is sometimes seen by the customer as the 'best' choice. To apply this technique successfully, you must listen carefully to the customer's comments so that the third possibility you offer is either a compromise between the two and becomes the 'best' choice, or is so markedly different from them that the customer's attention is concentrated on choosing one of the first two.

In the 'B' situation, the customer is spoiled for choice! There are so many possibilities that they have become obstacles to decision-making. You progress a 'B' situation by narrowing down the choice.

In general, you resolve 'A' situations by moving them towards a 'B' situation, and 'B' situations by bringing them back to an 'A' situation.

With the 'A' situation, that is when the customer has two equally attractive choices and cannot come to a decision, move it towards a 'B' situation: increase the choice with a third, and

CLOSING THE SALE 49

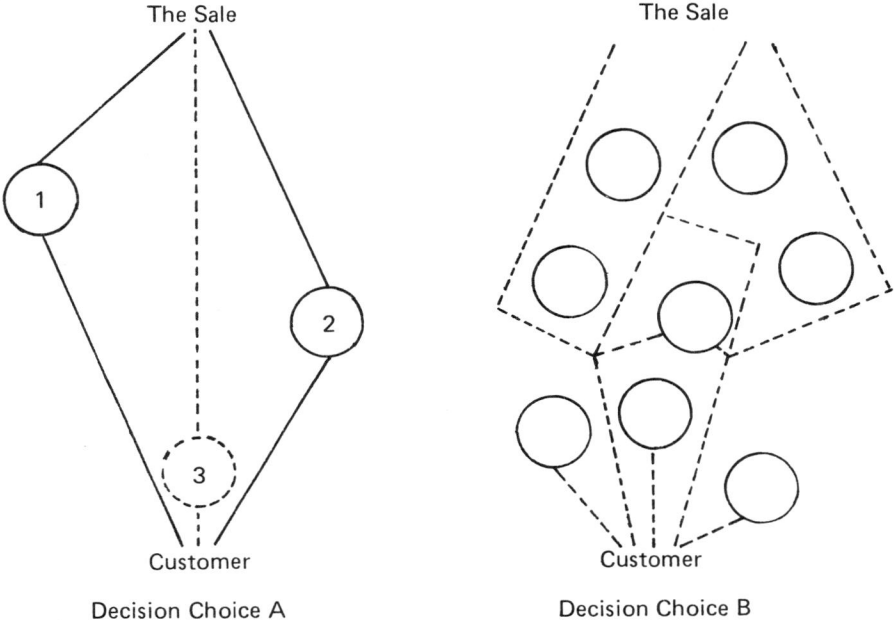

Decision Choice A   Decision Choice B

sometimes even a fourth possibility. If this third or fourth possibility is not then chosen as the 'best', a decision will normally be triggered toward one of the first two.

Confusion of choice

In the 'B' situation, the customer is faced with so many possible choices that he or she just doesn't know what to do: decision-making is blocked by the obstacles. Move the situation toward an 'A' situation. Remove all but two or three possibilities. Place those you remove well to one side and, at the same time, give sound reasons why you are removing them.

Saleswoman: This one (pointing to one) is not really the colour you wanted. This one (pointing to another) is a bit on the heavy side, I think, don't you? This (pointing to a third) I think would restrict your movement. This (pointing to a fourth) I think you might find difficult to keep clean...

To use this close, you must have listened carefully to what the customer has been saying so that you can 'play back' the various points he or she has made during your presentation.

The 'last one' close

'This is the last one we have.' 'This is the only one.' People tend to want what other want. This is an inborn human characteristic. Remove a child's toy that has not been touched for days or weeks and immediately you will get protests. If there is only one item left, and two people are interested in it, the fact that there is only one will increase their desire. The one who eventually gets it will feel lucky while the one who does not obtain it will feel unhappy.

If you say to a customer, 'I'm sorry but that one has been sold', the chances are that the customer will say that that is the very one wanted. You will have increased the customer's desire to acquire it! It is also human nature not to want to let an opportunity slip by.

Salesman: This is the last holdall at this price, I'm afraid, sir. If you don't like this colour, I haven't any more until the new stock arrives and they will be more expensive because of the change in the exchange rate.

This actually happened to the author when about to buy a new holdall in a London shop. The colour suddenly became very attractive at the old price!

Salesman: I think this one is sold. I'll just ask the buyer.

When you leave the customer for that few moments, it is only natural that the customer is hoping that it has not been sold.

Salesman: We've actually put that on one side for a customer but I'm not sure when she is coming in. If you'll wait a minute I'll find out. (After a short absence) Well, the supervisor says I can sell it if you really want it because the lady did say she was coming back on Monday and she was told we wouldn't keep it after then.

The desire to buy has been increased considerably.

CLOSING THE SALE 51

Saleswoman: Sorry, madam. This is the only size in this shade we have ordered this season.

You must remember that we are assuming that stock is restricted in styles, colours, shapes, models or whatever. It would be downright dishonest to tell a customer that it is the only one you have if there are, in fact, more in the back of the shop. The 'last one' close can only be used in those special circumstances. If you work in a department where the buyer obtains a range of sizes in selected colours and designs, so that there is a restricted range in shade, style and size, you are perfectly correct in using this close.

Closing on an objection

You must be careful not to use this form of closing until you are very experienced in your job. Where the customer is apparently satisfied with the product in all but one significant objection, and you know that you can deal with the objection satisfactorily, then this form of closing may be used.

Customer: Yes. I like it very much indeed.
Saleswoman: It does suit you.
Customer: Yes. It really is very nice. The colour is beautiful.
Saleswoman: Soft, too, isn't it?
Customer: Yes. There's just one thing. I don't like belts.
Saleswoman: (Says nothing)
Customer: It really does look very nice indeed. If it were only without the belt.
Saleswoman: Let me remove it a moment. (Does so)
Customer: There. See? It is much more attractive, isn't it?
Saleswoman: Yes. I'm bound to agree. Unbelted does look better on you.
Customer: Yes. Fine.

Barrier erecting

There are two very powerful selling techniques you can use in your sales presentation. One is known as 'barrier erecting', and the

52 RETAIL SELLING

other is restating an objection or a particular requirement made by the prospective buyer, and linking it with a product benefit.

Barrier erecting is repeating and agreeing facts made by the customer so that these cannot be subsequently denied. If the customer has stated a special requirement, you acknowledge this constraint by repeating it. The customer cannot afterwards retreat behind that statement.

For example, 'As you say, sir, it must be in red, otherwise you cannot use it', is a barrier behind which he cannot retreat. It has to be red—not pink or scarlet, but red.

Another: 'I agree with you, sir, it is essential to have a digital read-out if you wish to maintain absolute control over quality.' The barrier of the digital read-out means that the customer cannot subsequently say he would prefer it without.

Yet another: 'I understand completely, madam. You will have to obtain it today otherwise you will be in very serious difficulties.' The barrier erected here is the fact that the purchase has to be made that day. The woman cannot subsequently say that she will wait until tomorrow.

Linking with a benefit

The second technique, restating the condition, objection or problem, should only be used when you know that you have a product that will deal with this, or will satisfy the special requirement stipulated by the customer. Let's see this in the case of the woman and the coat without the belt. We left the woman putting the coat on with the belt removed from its retaining straps.

Saleswoman: Yes. I'm bound to agree. Unbelted does look better on you.
Customer: Yes. Fine.
Saleswoman: That coat without the belt is what you really want. (Statement more than a question)
Customer: Oh yes!
Saleswoman: If we have one in the same shade and your size in stock, you would like to take it?
Customer: Certainly.

And the sale is closed because there was one in stock but, and this

CLOSING THE SALE

is the important point, *the saleswoman knew it.* When you use this technique of repeating what has been objected to or what has been stipulated, you must know that you have a product that will answer the objection or satisfy the stipulated requirement.

Consider the situation of the man who stated that the machine must have a digital read-out. The salesman knew that he had a product that would satisfy this requirement but he did not jump in and say so immediately.

He restated the buyer's requirement first. But also he erected the barrier. He was using both techniques at the same time.

A slight variation on the 'unbelted coat' close is to combine it with the 'last one' close.

Saleswoman: Another customer made exactly the same observation. We did put the only unbelted model on one side for her but I think it's gone. I'm not sure though. I think it was your size. Just a moment, I'll have a look in the stockroom.

Imagine the desire being built up in the customer! But do not oversell. If you use these techniques use them quietly and naturally as though you do it every day—as indeed you should be!

Ask for the order

Never be afraid of asking for the order. You are there to give service to customers and you will not offend the vast majority if you say, 'Do you want to take it today, sir?' What you are actually asking is 'Do you want to buy it?' but to put the question in this way would be rather rude so you frame your 'asking for the order' question quite naturally. Another suggestion: 'Well, that seems to cover everything, madam. Shall I make out the bill?'

Modifying the product

Finally, a close you may find very useful at times is altering or modifying the product to satisfy the customer's wishes. This does not necessarily mean sending it to the workroom or back to the manufacturer. It could be as simple as removing a belt from a coat and taking off the straps to retain it. It could mean removing an artificial flower from a dress or a piece of over-embellishment from a hat. You could remove the automatic sheet-feed from an electronic typewriter and reduce the price accordingly.

With this close, take care that you know what the store will alter without charge and what has to be charged to the customer. If a skirt is too long for a customer and it needs shortening, there will most likely be a charge, especially if it is a pleated skirt because there is a lot of work involved. Make sure that your customer knows that there will be a charge; don't assume this. Say something along the lines of 'I think this garment is worth spending a little extra on to get it just right'.

If your shop is selling expensive products there may be no charge for alterations and modifications, but check in advance so that you do not have to seek advice at the time of closing the sale. It spoils the presentation and, if you have to leave the customer to find out, the customer may have had a change of mind by the time you return!

Summarizing the closing techniques:

- The 'yes' close.
- Implying by word and/or action that the customer will buy.
- Closing on a minor point.
- Narrowing the choice.
- The 'last one' or 'the only one' close.
- Objection closing.
- Asking for the order.
- Offer to modify or alter the product.

5
The Power of Enthusiasm

Enthusiasm is persuasive

You can't help being influenced by someone who enthusiastically describes something.

> 'Oh! It's a fabulous place. The climate's superb and the hotel is just, well, incredible!'
> 'I wouldn't use any other. I've had mine now for nearly ten years. It never lets me down.'
> 'You should see it! So clean, and everything to hand.'
> 'I can't speak too highly of them. Their service is faultless.'
> 'I've had several different makes before, but this one is absolutely superb. I wouldn't change it.'
> 'You could pay twice the price, but you wouldn't get it any better.'
> 'Oh. Since I've started using it, I never have any of the old problems.'

Enthusiasm relates to a highly favourable judgement of something with few, if any, reservations. It does not need to be loud and abrasive but can be projected quietly with warmth and affection.

Don't be a misery

No one likes to be served by a sales assistant who doesn't seem to care, or appears to have the whole world of troubles on his or her shoulders. You probably know of some shops where you avoid being served by a particular person because that person always appears to be miserable.

It's very easy to take personal and private problems into the store and unknowingly transmit them to your customers. If you have such problems, discuss them with the appropriate person in your company. Don't let them fester in the background.

Not many of us are at our best first thing in the morning and this can sometimes extend to the first hour or so when we meet the early customers. The way to overcome our early morning 'blues' is to be interested in the customers' problems.

Why people buy

People buy for their reasons, not for yours. They do not buy for your store's sake or for that of the suppliers or manufacturers of the products. They buy because they have their own personal reasons. No matter how many reasons you have for believing that your products are first class, these mean nothing unless the customer has her or his own reasons for wanting to buy from you.

To find out those reasons is not easy. Yet, if you concentrate on the customer's problems and really try to find out why they want to do business with you, success will usually follow.

The very fact that you search out these reasons will create an atmosphere of enthusiasm. You are interested in people; you are interested in their problems; you are interested in finding out their real reasons for wanting to buy.

Salesman:	Good morning, sir.	
Customer:	Good morning.	
Salesman:	(Says nothing else but waits for the customer)	
Customer:	Awful weather; got soaked walking from the car.	
Salesman:	Yes, sir. I sometimes wonder how accurate the weather forecasts really are.	
Customer:	I'm looking for — not quite sure what you call it. I've got a problem with our washing machine. The connectors leak.	
Salesman:	Connectors to the water supply?	
Customer:	Yes.	
Salesman:	Are they connected to both hot and cold water supply?	
Customer:	No. Just the cold water tap; there's no hot water connection.	
Salesman:	Where exactly is the leak?	

THE POWER OF ENTHUSIASM 57

Customer: At the tap and between the connectors. It sprays water like a shower. Got worse over the last couple of weeks.

Salesman: You said, 'connectors', but there is just one supply from the cold water tap to the washing machine.

Customer: Yes.

Salesman: (Enthusiastically) Oh. We'll, I don't think we'll have too much trouble trying to help you. How old is the machine?

Customer: Not old. We've had it about a year or so.

Salesman: And the tap?

Customer: Probably as old as the house. Very old.

Salesman: Does it have a screw at the nozzle?

Customer: Yes. That's where it's leaking.

Salesman: Does the screw-end of the hose from the washing machine fit directly on to the tap or is there a connector between the hose and the tap?

Customer: There's a connector.

Salesman: That's because your tap is old and has a larger screw than the screw at the end of the hose. That connector is a reducer; it enables a smaller screw to be fitted to a larger one. Have you taken it apart?

Customer: No. I've tried to tighten it.

Salesman: Without seeing the connector, I can't be absolutely sure, but I think your problem is that the washers are worn. It's only recently that you've been getting a shower with the washing?

Customer: (Laughing) Yes.

Salesman: Old taps with a screw-end are all 30 millimetre diameter; the modern ones are 25. You probably need a couple of new washers— 30mm and 25mm. Remove the old ones and fit these. Of course, if I'm wrong, let me have them back. I could ask you to bring the connector in, but this may save you a journey.

The salesman wasn't feeling 'on top of the world' just before the customer came in. He isn't going to make a high profit sale but, by being genuinely interested in the customer's problem, he is already feeling better. This is enthusiasm at work.

Everyone has problems

We usually think that our problems are bigger and more difficult than anyone else's. This is natural, simply because they are *our* problems. But, don't tell customers your problems; listen to theirs. They are much more important.

By taking a genuine interest in your customers' problems, and relating these to your range of products, you can help to solve them. They will be happy; you will feel happy. Already, you are working at being enthusiastic in your job.

Enthusiasm has to be worked at

We do not wake up every day 'feeling on top of the world'. Most days are like every other day: same routine, more difficulties, new problems, the usual batch of awkward customers... It's not easy to be enthusiastic. But enthusiasm is not something with which we are born. We have to work at it. To be enthusiastic means to have an ardent zeal for something. This means being interested in things, in our job, in our products and in the people we meet.

There are some fundamentals that help to create enthusiasm. We should have a good home life, good health, plenty of energy, enjoy our work and possess knowledge. It is possible, of course, to be enthusiastic about something even if we are not feeling well or if we suffer from some disability. But, generally speaking, if we have a poor family life, dislike our job, and are unenergetic, then no matter how knowledgeable we may be, we are unlikely to be very enthusiastic.

Think positively and not negatively, and you will increase your ability to be enthusiastic. Think 'yes' things rather than 'no' things and your general attitude will be positive. You meet a colleague:

    You: Good morning.
    Colleague: What's good about it?

That makes you feel fine, doesn't it! You don't want to spend more time than necessary with such a happy person! And you certainly won't waste much time trying to find out why they are so miserable.

Obviously, you wouldn't speak like that with a customer, but the tone of your voice, the words you use or the general lack of sparkle will just as quickly transmit a 'what's good about it?' to the customer.

Secret of enthusiasm

The source of enthusiasm is rooted in confidence. Confidence in what you are selling, confidence in handling customers. This means you must learn a lot about your products: where they are made; how they are made; what they are capable of doing; how they can be used by customers.

You must learn a lot about your customers: their general tendencies; how they approach you; the many ways in which they ask the same question; their reluctance or inability to express themselves; their need of help in establishing their real needs; their willingness to buy, or to delay buying.

When you have made yourself thoroughly conversant with your products, you are able to cope with most situations concerning them. You are able to explain things to your customers, show them how to get the best out of a product, answer their questions. This is where enthusiasm is rooted. Without such knowledge, you cannot be confident, and without confidence, you cannot be enthusiastic.

You still have to work at being enthusiastic. Knowing your products thoroughly will not automatically make you confident and enthusiastic. However, the reverse is true: lack of knowledge and confidence makes it almost impossible to be enthusiastic.

Value of knowledge

Acquiring knowledge has to be worked at; it doesn't just arrive. It means maintaining an enquiring mind to expand your knowledge and, thus, your confidence. Don't be satisfied with just sufficient information to get by. Find out all you can about your products and, where possible, about your competitors' products. Aim to become an expert in them. You'll find that even your colleagues will start asking your advice.

60 RETAIL SELLING

Your health

Your body is important to you because retail selling can be an arduous job and requires healthy people. You will probably be on your feet many hours a day and, in the course of your work, walk many miles. For this reason alone, you will be getting a lot of exercise.

You will meet an endless stream of customers, all apparently with the same questions, same monotony, same tediousness. At least, that is what it will appear to be if you are feeling 'one degree under'. While it is not intended to deal with a guide to health in this book, and you cannot feel 'on top of the world' all the time, there are some simple guidelines to follow.

Be prudent in your general habits insofar as they may have an impact on your customers. Shower or bath every morning to prevent unpleasant body odour; be aware that, if you smoke, your breath will be unpleasant to non-smokers. If you drink midday, be sure that it is the nearly non-alcohol type: alcoholic breath is also unpleasant for customers.

Listen constantly to customers

To help you in your relations with other people, *listen.* Listen to what they say and how they say it. Don't let your thoughts run all over the place when a customer is talking. Listen to what is being said and wait until the person has stopped speaking.

Act like a recorder; record what is being said and be able to repeat it. If you can develop this habit of listening, you will find that you become a much more acceptable person. A strange thing will happen to you when you constantly listen to others. People will think that you are a charming person and that you have a nice character. The reason? You're interested in them!

People are interested in themselves

When you show someone a photograph of a group of people, what do they look for? For you? For friends? For the tallest person in the group? No! Of course not. They look for themselves.

Use this idea when you listen to people. Ask them where *they* stand, what do *they* think, how did *they* act and what did *they* do.

THE POWER OF ENTHUSIASM   61

Your personality will begin to grow in step with the interest you take in other people. Your enthusiasm will grow with it!

By considering yourself you will develop a good and energetic body. By considering others, you will develop a happy atmosphere and a happy feeling for your job. You are looking after your most vital possession—your physical and mental health.

Knowledge of words

A knowledge of words is also something you have to work at. Your selling tools are your voice and speech. You will sound enthusiastic if you talk about your products with understanding and feeling. This means using words that convey the right impression to the customer.

Occasionally use words that are not heard in everyday speech; but don't use words that are so rare that the customer needs a dictionary to understand you.

Avoid using overworked words and phrases: they are like overworked people—tired, dull and uncommunicative.

Don't use 'lovely', 'beautiful', 'nice', or 'super' too often, and avoid using phrases such as 'it's a bargain' and 'we sell a lot of them'. Use words that are appropriate and descriptive.

Clichés

Clichés are overworked phrases. We hear them every day and, because they are so familiar, they fail to have any meaning. Here are some that are over-used in retail selling; try to avoid them:

   the object of the exercise (explaining some apparatus)
   much of a muchness (comparing two items)
   few and far between (trying to stress the rarity of a product)
   you've hit the nail on the head (agreeing with a customer's statement)
   six of one and half a dozen of the other (comparing two items)
   the object of the exercise (explaining use of a product)
   part and parcel (describing separate parts of a product)
   slow but sure (commenting on product's working)
   short and sweet (explaining duration of product's working)

62 RETAIL SELLING

selling like hot cakes (explaining rate of sales of a product)
cool as a cucumber (describing what the product does)
dead as a doornail (comparing an old with a new product)
smooth as silk (describing a product's feature)
right as rain (stressing result of using a product)
flat as a pancake (describing a product's use)
stick out like a sore thumb (an old product's feature)
know what I mean? (asking if customer understands)
over the moon (describing other customers' reactions)
like muck off a blanket (describing speed of operation)
take a pew (offering a chair)
at the end of the day (finally)
in the pipeline (a new product is due)
in this day and age (the customer's previous product is old-fashioned)
a proven track record (the manufacturer is very experienced)
at this point in time (now)

Sales sentences

Make a note of any sales sentences you use that you find descriptive and useful in your presentations. Here are a few statements about a domestic washing machine used by a saleswoman in a department store:

The programmes are comprehensive: they seem to have thought of everything.
The programmes have been very well designed.
You can programme it for all your needs.
There are ten programmes—they'll cover all your needs.
The programming is sophisticated but very easy to use.
You won't find a more versatile machine at the price.

Vocabulary and salary

Some years ago, a study was made of certain American university graduates prior to their graduation and, subsequently, in their employment about three years after leaving university. Without exception, there was a high correlation between the size of their salaries and the size of their vocabularies.

THE POWER OF ENTHUSIASM

Practice

Like everything else worth doing, you must practise the use of words and 'break them in' as you would a new pair of shoes. You cannot develop a skilful and accurate use of words overnight. Learn a new word every week, not every day. You would be undertaking a task that you couldn't maintain. One new word a week will mean that not only will you know what it means, and know how to use it, but it will become part of *your* vocabulary.

Case Study: The Lightweight Sale

Joan King worked in a children's department of a store in the midlands region of the UK and was having a rather boring day with very little custom.

A smartly dressed woman walked into the department and started to look through the rack of dresses for the 'under tens'. Joan walked quickly toward the customer and said, 'Good afternoon, madam', then, taking hold of the pretty dress that the customer was holding commented, 'It's sweet, isn't it?'

'Hm!' mumbled the customer and turned to look at the other end of the display.

'Here's a very attractive dress,' enthused Joan. 'It's in nylon and will wash very well. Do you like the pink shade?'

'I'm not really sure what I want,' ventured the woman, 'I'm just looking at the moment. I think I'll leave it for the time being. Thank you.'

'While I'm here,' continued the woman, 'I'd like to see some dressing gowns.'

'Certainly,' replied Joan, pointing in the general direction of another department where her friend Linda Mason worked, 'through the arch and on the left.'

'Which arch?' asked the visitor. 'There appear to be two.'

'I'll show you,' said Joan. She then led the woman through her department, through an archway, down a small flight of stairs to the department where Linda was standing. 'Hey, Linda,' called Joan softly, 'can you serve this customer?' She then left but, on the stairs, turned and grimaced to Linda behind the woman's back as she returned to her own department.

'I'm looking for a lightweight gown suitable for travelling,' said the customer. Linda smiled, and led her to a display rack and selected a blue nylon with trimmings of lace and ribbons.

'I think this is a beautiful gown,' she said. 'It's reasonably priced, too. Very light and shouldn't crease when packed.'

64 RETAIL SELLING

'I think I prefer something a little more practical,' said the customer, 'warm yet lightweight.'

'This nylon gown would be very warm, madam, and it will pack very easily.'

'No!' The customer looked a little disappointed. 'Don't you have some lightweight woollen ones?'

'We have these,' said Linda. 'They're a little dated, I think, but they're warm. They're quite expensive.'

'Are they pure wool?'

'Oh! I'm sure they are at that price,' laughed Linda. 'Of course, they're made by a well-known maker and are lovely and soft. They're £45, I'm afraid.'

'That's quite enough, I suppose,' said the customer.

'Oh! We have some cheaper ones,' responded Linda. 'Here is a brushed 'Acrilan'. These are in a wonderful range of colours and are only £15.'

Linda had now arranged several dressing gowns on the counter in front of the woman, who was obviously undecided as to which she preferred.

Another customer walked hurriedly into the department looking rather impatient. Linda said to her first customer, who was picking up the gowns in turn, 'I'll just see to this lady, if I may. She seems to be in a hurry. Do you mind?' And, without waiting for an answer, she said 'good afternoon' to the person who had just arrived.

'I'm looking for — dresses,' said the woman quickly, mentioning the name of a well-known maker, 'do you stock them?'

'I'm sorry, no, madam,' said Linda quickly. 'You'll find them at Smith's along the high street. They stock that brand.' She then turned to her first customer in time to see her walking out of the department.

1. Was the first woman a customer or not? How should Joan have approached her? Why do you think that Joan took hold of the dress that the customer was holding?
2. What went wrong in this store? (Perhaps it might be easier if you said what went right!) If you had been Joan, how would you have introduced the customer to Linda? If you had been Linda, how would you have acted when your friend Joan brought the customer in? What action do you consider that Linda should have taken when the impatient customer walked in?

6
Determining the Approach

The approach

Whether or not you have to approach customers in your store, that is, actually walk toward them and speak, will depend on the layout of the store. If you stand behind a counter, customers will approach you. If your store has island displays and/or counters, you may need to approach customers physically.

In the selling sense, however, the 'approach' is the way that a possible sales presentation is started. It is a combination of saying 'good morning', or whatever, and how to open the sale.

Think of this approach in the same way that you approach a roundabout in a car. You have to take up a position on the road as you approach it depending on whether you intend to turn left, go straight on, or take a subsequent turning off the roundabout.

So it is with the sales approach. You are not actually on the roundabout, that is, into your sales presentation; you are about to approach it. Your potential customer may simply be looking at products and comparing your prices and qualities with those of goods seen in other stores.

Suspects and prospects

A useful tip can be taken from sales people who travel in their work, calling on customers and potential customers in a given area. They distinguish between suspects and prospects. If they see a large office or factory they may think that there is an opportunity to offer their products for sale. Until they find out what that company is doing, it remains a suspect; that is, it is not a prospective customer.

A prospect is a person (or company) who can both benefit from buying the product and can afford to buy it. These two conditions must be satisfied before a suspect can be classified as being a prospect.

You are at an advantage over the travelling sales person because people who visit your store can, in general, be classified as prospects. They know your range of goods and they have a good idea of prices. However, they may still be suspects because they may not be willing to buy at that time. If you have a restaurant in your store, a lot of its clients will wander round the store on their way out, looking at the displays of goods.

You can see how important the approach is. The sales presentation is comparatively easy because an interest has been expressed. The approach needs careful consideration.

When to approach customers

Knowing how and when to approach prospective customers will increase your chances of making sales. It will also help to maintain a good image for your store. By observing customers and putting the appropriate questions you can adjust your sales presentations to their real needs.

 Salesman: Good morning, madam, may I help you?
 Customer: No, thank you; I'm just looking around.

Not a very useful start. The customer did not need help at that time and the premature approach by the salesman might subsequently stop her from seeking advice. The customer has said 'no' once and may be reluctant to ask for even the most minor information in case the salesman starts to 'sell her something'! A small barrier has been created between the seller and the buyer by the premature approach. Customers are often self-conscious when shopping. Notice how many of them put a hand to their face, near the mouth, when asking you a question. This is an unconscious gesture—'body language'—wishing to put the question as quietly as possible.

There is no need to ask a customer, 'Can I help you?' That is what you are there for and, as the customer has visited you, what she or he expects from you. It is better for the customer to decide when help is required from a sales person.

The best approach

The best way of approaching a potential customer (or a suspect customer) is to look them in the eyes and smile. You don't even need to say 'good morning', or 'good afternoon'; just smile. This tells the customer that you know they are there and are ready to give assistance if needed. Don't give help until you have been asked or it is obvious that help is needed; don't give opinions before you have heard the customer's opinion!

> Salesman: (To customer looking at a display of ties) Attractive, aren't they, sir. Is there any particular design or colour you're looking for?
> Customer: No, thank you. I think they're more suitable for the Caribbean beach; they're a bit loud, aren't they!

Whoops! Not a good approach either. The salesman obviously thought that because the customer was looking at the rack of ties he was interested in buying one. Never assume that a customer who is looking at a display of goods is going to buy something. If you misread a customer's intentions it can disturb an otherwise agreeable presentation; if you take the customer's view for granted, it can destroy all chances of making a sale.

The following dialogue took place between the author and a salesman in a car distributor's showroom at Kidlington, just north of Oxford. I had no intention of making the salesman feel ill at ease, but his breezy manner and faulty approach prompted me to explore his selling skills.

> Author: (Enters showroom and stops at one particular new model and starts looking at bodywork and interior)
> Salesman: (Walking briskly, heels clicking, down the showroom to the author) Good afternoon, sir. Can I help you?
> Author: (Acts startled) Pardon?
> Salesman: Can I help you?
> Author: (As though surprised) Help me? (Slight pause) Help me to do what?
> Salesman: Er—no—er—can I help you?
> Author: Oh! (Apparently realizing the meaning of the question) Well, I don't know. What d'you want to help me with?

Salesman:	(Obviously thinks he is dealing with a nut) Um! Well, no. Is there anything you'd like to know about the car?
Author:	(Pauses) I'm not sure. I've only just arrived. As soon as I started looking at it, you came.

The salesman was unable to develop the presentation and, having started with the cliché 'Can I help you?', had put himself at a disadvantage. Had he been adequately trained, he would not have approached me until the right moment.

By marching down the showroom with guardsman-like heel clicks and tackling a possible customer in this way, the salesman effectively damaged his opportunity to obtain the customer's interest.

Don't be a highwayman

In olden days, travellers, especially those in stage-coaches, were often in danger of being stopped at gunpoint by highwaymen who would rob them of money and valuables. The cry of these highway marauders as they pointed their pistols and held up a stage-coach was, 'Stand and deliver!'

This is exactly like the untrained sales person who directs a verbal pistol at a potential customer: 'Can I help you?', 'Is there something you want?', 'Tell me if you're going to buy something, otherwise don't waste my time!'

Don't 'hold up' your possible customers. Don't ask them to stand and deliver. Put them at ease. Learn how and when to approach them.

Don't stand on guard

The opposite of bearing down on a customer, verbal pistol at the ready, is to stand guard over a display of products. Do this, preferably, with the arms folded and feet slightly apart. This stance is guaranteed to ward off any unsuspecting customers who venture near to the display. You can reinforce it with a sardonic smile that warns them, 'Disturb or touch this display at your peril!'

Knowing your customers

After you have been selling for some time in the same store, you will get to know a lot of customers and become well acquainted with some of them. You will remember names and faces. However, most of your customers will be strangers and you must decide how best to approach each sale. Let us review the points made so far to see exactly what we mean by approach.

What takes place in the customer's mind when a sale is made can occur quickly, in a matter of 20 or 30 seconds, or over a period of minutes, even hours or days. There are six stages:

1. I shall ask this sales assistant.
2. I shall listen to what the assistant has to say.
3. I understand what the assistant is saying and will judge whether the offer will benefit me.
4. I approve the proposition.
5. I will accept the offer.
6. I will act now.

These six customer decisions are fundamental. Most sales involve the majority of them. The period of time may be quite small between any two of them but, nevertheless, most of these stages occur when a sale is made. The first two stages will take place if your approach is appropriate to the prospective customer.

Objectives of a good approach

The objectives of a good approach are:

- To gain the customer's attention.
- To awaken the customer's interest in the proposition.
- To lead in to the sales presentation.

Sometimes the approach, sales presentation, suggestion and persuasion all merge into one over a comparatively short period of time.

Salesman: (Cheerily, in a bright voice, to customer who walks into the car accessory shop) Good morning, sir. How may I help you?

Customer: I need some hose. (Producing a sample) This burst on my way home last night. I had to stop five times and fill up with water.

70 RETAIL SELLING

Salesman: Yep! It looks as though it's done its job. (Looks at the hose closely) You had a job getting it off, I think!
Customer: You're right. How d'you know?
Salesman: It's the original hose and these marks (pointing) were made when it was fitted in the factory. Here's a piece of new hose (places new hose on counter) and I think you'll find it easier to work with a couple of new clips. (Places two clips beside the hose)
Customer: Fine.
Salesman: You say you lost the water?
Customer: Yes. Had to stop and fill up five times.
Salesman: So you'll need to replace your antifreeze.
Customer: Yes. I suppose you're right.
Salesman: Well, while the system's drained, it's a good idea to flush it through with a cleaner. How old's the car?
Customer: About five years.
Salesman: Now's your chance to clean out the rust. After you've replaced the hose, my advice is to put this tin through (places product on counter) with about a gallon of water, then flush it out and fill it up with the new antifreeze and fresh water.
Customer: Fine. I think we'd better stop there!

The right approach, linked with a good sales presentation, helps you to make friends with the customer and helps the customer to buy.

Eight ways to open the sale

You will remember that we discussed eight ways of opening a sale:
- Introductory approach
- Product approach
- Curiosity opening
- Shock opening
- Statement opening
- Premium opening
- Compliment approach
- Question opening

DETERMINING THE APPROACH

You will probably find that the most widely used are the question, compliment, curiosity and statement openings. As we have seen, the question opening is probably the most fruitful for leading in to the presentation. What you have to determine when you meet a prospective customer who is a stranger to you, is what kind of approach is most likely to succeed.

Observation is useful

Use your eyes and ears to observe the prospect. First, observe the person: male or female; young or old; well-spoken or not; used to issuing instructions or not; knows what's wanted or not; looks 'well-off', average, shabby or of undetermined financial status.

Be careful about making judgements based on people's dress. Don't be misled by the suggestion that the more money people have, the less conscious they are about their dress. Also, many people dress quite well but have heavy expenses and little money available for luxuries.

The reason for this initial observation is to help decide how best to approach and open the sale. There are no rules to guide you; you must learn by your own experience. Observing customers builds your experience.

Three types of customer

Customers generally fall into three main types: those in the 'willing to spend money' category; those who are unwilling to spend money; and those who leave you in doubt.

For example, if a well dressed woman walked up to you and said, 'I'd like to see some unlined, soft leather gloves please, size six and a half, in a darkish brown similar to my coat,' you would probably place her in the first category—willing to spend money.

You must decide on the best way to open the sales presentation because the customer has already opened by asking to see something. Obviously we can dispense with the question and shock openings as they are both inappropriate, as are the premium and the compliment openings. The best opening is obviously a combination of the product and the statement with the accent on the product and a 'soft pedal' on the statement.

Reason for buying

When a customer does not give a clear indication of what is wanted, then you must explore with questions. Remember that no one buys a product for itself alone, but for the satisfaction it gives. Therefore, if it is appropriate, ask the purpose for which the product is to be used; what quantity is required; what kind of material is desired. In other words, find out what it is the customer is hoping to satisfy by the acquisition of the product.

You must decide whether the customer is interested in economy or status; quality or low outlay; the initial payment or the running or operating costs. Often it is better to buy what requires a higher initial payment but which is less costly to operate or to run.

Observe, question, and listen

Ask questions to determine what the customer really needs. Observe the customer to determine how you will open your sales and develop the sales presentation. Listen carefully to all responses.

What will be running through the customer's mind will be the first two stages in the buying process: 'I will ask this sales person' and 'I will listen to what is said'. By your greeting, you can convince the customer that the first stage is worth taking and the way in which you open the sale will convince the customer that the second stage is worth taking.

Let the product sell itself

Once you have decided on the approach and started the sale, you will find it helpful to let the product sell itself. No amount of words and description can take the place of the product.

When you are showing the product cut your talk to an absolute minimum. This really is important. Let the customer look at the product, feel it, hold it, try it on or put it into use, but keep your words to the barest essentials.

If a man is being shown a camera, hand it to him at the appropriate moment and say nothing but watch to see if he needs guidance in using it.

If the customer is feeling, say, a pure lambswool scarf, look at

DETERMINING THE APPROACH 73

the customer and say earnestly, 'It's very soft.' There is no need to say 'Isn't it beautifully made? Isn't it soft? What a lovely colour!', because the customer will not really hear you. As the customer handles the scarf the word 'soft' is the only one that matters.

Supposing the customer puts it around her neck. She will want to look at herself in a mirror. Indicate the nearest one. When she looks at her reflection, if you feel you must say something, ask 'Do you like the shade?' or 'Does it have to tone with any special colour?'

Do not fall into the trap of saying something about the 'lovely colour' or 'beautiful shade', or that it suits her, because you do not know at that point whether she likes it.

When to comment

Comments may be objective or subjective. Objective comments are independent of opinion. They are factual comments:

> This is the smallest programmable short-wave radio on the market.
> This is a heavy, two-ply cashmere; that one is single-ply.
> It's a universal fitting; it adjusts to any outlet.
> The spin-speed is the highest of any machine.
> It has an automatic non-return valve; the water supply cannot be polluted.
> That is one of the new season's colours.

Subjective comments are opinions expressed by someone. They tell the listener what you think and are not necessarily factual.

> It's a very handy radio for the traveller.
> This is the better quality cardigan.
> I always use these; they're so adaptable.
> I like to get my clothes really dry; you can with this one.
> That's an extra gadget if you need it.
> It's a gorgeous colour.

Find out what the customer thinks about a product before you make any subjective comment. You are not there to give your opinions on products; you are there to help customers to buy. Your tastes and feeling for products cannot possibly be the same as every customer you serve. Therefore, you must not voice your feelings but rather reflect what the customer says.

If the customer has selected something that you are convinced is unsuitable, should you say so or not?

Obviously you have a duty to your customer to give sound, unbiased advice. If the electrical apparatus is not suitable but the customer thinks it is; if you doubt that the accessory will work adequately on the customer's present equipment; if the jacket is too long or too short—all these require you to state objective advice. You must tell the customer. If you are not sure, seek a second opinion from one of your colleagues before you say anything to the customer.

If it is a question of taste or personal preference, that is, if a subjective comment is required, you should reflect the customer's opinion and not yours.

If you give your subjective comment first and the customer disagrees, you are then on opposite sides. Wait until you know what the customer thinks, then you can reinforce the customer's opinion with a suitably worded comment.

7
Buying Motives and Selling Points

Selling points

All products have characteristics or attributes: their size, shape, feel, weight, style and design. If the product is a piece of equipment or some apparatus, the list includes speed and ease of working, simplicity of use, cost of operating, accessibility for cleaning and many other things.

Some of these attributes give benefits to the customer. A raincoat for warm weather that is lightweight is obviously better than a heavy one; a dress that does not readily crease and is easily cleaned is ideal for travelling; a power drill with variable speed and a hammer device for masonry work is more versatile than a fixed speed drill.

However, not all product attributes are potential customer benefits. The author once experienced a difficult meeting with a client concerning a new product attribute that was not a customer benefit and described it in *Selling by Telephone* (1986, Kogan Page, pp 49-50).

> Some years ago I was handling the marketing for a large company, one of whose factories made carpet sweepers. These are pushed across the carpet on their rubber wheels that revolve and turn brushes that flick up the dirt into the container inside the cleaner. Very useful when you have power cuts and crumbs and dirt on the carpets!
>
> When visiting the sales director one day he asked me to look at the latest improvement in the carpet sweeper handle. He gave me the new handle and said, 'Look at the screw.'
>
> The end of the handle that screwed into the cleaner body had an aluminium thread on it. This company had always fixed aluminium threads on the handles in preference to a screw turned in the actual wood of the handle.
>
> 'Yes,' I said, 'it's got an aluminium screw.'

'You don't understand, do you!' he remonstrated. 'It's been moulded on. Not fixed as before—moulded. Moulded onto the end. It'll never come off. I've just got it from the factory about half-an-hour ago.'

'I can't see any difference,' I confessed.

'It's moulded,' he shouted, 'moulded onto the wood. We used to fix them with small screws. That moulded screw-end will always be part of the handle. The aluminium is now part of the wood.'

'I can just see the advertising,' I said, '"Our handles have moulded screw-ends. They'll never come off!" But the handles never came off before. What's new about this? I'm sorry, Bill, I think it's fine. It's a great achievement in the factory but it's simply a product attribute. You haven't any additional benefit for the user because she didn't have any problems with loose handles before.'

I went on to recount that my grandmother had a competitive carpet sweeper made by Ewbank. Very, very old. Yet, although it had an ordinary turned thread in the wood to screw into the body of the cleaner, it had never given any trouble in about thirty years!

Like the bearer of bad news to potentates of old, I was not very popular that day. Nevertheless, to avoid facing the truth then would only have stored up problems for later on.

Make sure that you know all the attributes of your products and then decide which of these are customer benefits. A lot of these benefits will also be benefits of competitive products. Finding benefits that are unique to your products is not easy. Your buyers may help, because they may have bought those products because of the unique benefits. Also, your store may even have some products specially produced.

Unique selling points

Sometimes, the search for unique product benefits backfires. One day, when I was employed with Moss Bros, the chain of men's and women's outfitters, Harry Moss called me into his office and said, 'I see that Marks and Spencers are selling a white tunic shirt at 25/11 (£1.30). We are selling at—what?'

'Ours are two guineas,' I replied.

'But they are substantially the same shirt,' he exclaimed. 'Why should anyone pay us over £2 for much the same shirt they can get from Marks and Spencer for 26 shillings?'

'Ah! I said, 'But ours have the Moss Bros label in them.'

He was not impressed. 'Do you think anyone is going to come up from south of London to Covent Garden and pay us two guineas

BUYING MOTIVES AND SELLING POINTS

for a shirt with our label, when they can get the same thing for much less from any Marks' store?'

I had to admit that the unique product benefit diminished rapidly in face of his argument. His further remarks were also important to retail selling.

'If you can't compete on price,' he proclaimed, 'don't even try. We should stock a much better shirt.' We subsequently stocked a very fine weave cotton shirt at twice our original price and it sold well.

Buying points

A selling point describes a product attribute from the viewpoint of the seller. If you intend to be a really good sales person, it is better to consider selling points as buying points. Similarly, unique selling points are better considered as unique buying points. Your task is to relate these buying points to the customers' motives for buying.

Buying motives

There are many reasons why people buy particular goods and products. Mostly they know their reasons for buying; sometimes, they don't. Quite often, they see a product which attracts them, and devise a buying motive for it.

Your task, generally, is to relate selling points to buying motives. If you discover that the customer has no immediate motive for buying, obviously you cannot relate the selling points to anything. You must then make the customer's desire to possess the article greater than the money it costs.

The following conversation took place between a couple of visitors and the owner of an antique shop in Cornwall.

Owner:	Good morning.
Customers:	Good morning. We're just having a look round.
Owner:	By all means.
Customer 1:	That's a nice plate (pointing) on the wall there.
Owner:	Ah! Yes, indeed. There's been quite a bit of interest in that.

Customer 2: What's the price?
Owner: (Removing plate and rack from wall and handing it to the customer) My lowest price for it is £38.
Customer 1: (Gives a whistle)
Customer 2: (Looking at plate) There's a price ticket on it for £43.
Owner: £38 is my lowest trade price.
Customer 2: (To customer 1) I don't understand.
Customer 1: (To customer 2) It's the normal practice. The price on the article is usually for tourists.
Customer 2: But we are—
Customer 1: (Cutting the other short and to owner) It seems a lot of money.
Owner: It's a genuine Minton. (Taking plate from customer and turning it over) See here; here's the impression. That's the Minton mark. You won't find many of these around. That's why, as I say, there's been quite a bit of interest in it.
Customer 2: (To customer 1) It's nice. I like it.
Customer 1: But where would you put it? I mean, do you really need it? You don't collect Minton.
Customer 2: No! But you can say that of many things. It's very nice.
Customer 1: It's a lot of money, £38.

The owner offered no further help or advice and did not seem particularly interested whether the plate was purchased or not. The two visitors left without buying and yet, with a little effort, the owner could have made the sale. I know, because I was the unconvinced customer. I tried to buy it a couple of weeks later as a present for my colleague; it had been sold!

If you want to sell your products and merchandise, find out the customer's buying motives and link these with the various buying points in a way that will satisfy those motives. If there appear to be no immediate buying motives, explore the reasons why the customer is interested in the product.

Selling and buying are the same thing

There can be no selling without buying! This is a simple fact that

BUYING MOTIVES AND SELLING POINTS

we often forget. Selling and buying are not adversaries, one fighting the other. Selling and buying describe the same thing. A customer might say to a friend, 'I've just bought this coat.' The salesman, who sold the coat, could just as easily say to a colleague, 'I've just sold that coat.'

Yet, they are both describing the same event. Buying and selling are simply different views of the same transaction.

A sale is made, not over the counter, not in the mind of the sales person, not by hard selling or pushing products, but *in the mind of the buyer*.

Everything you do when selling should be to make the right impression on the customer's mind.

Customers' backgrounds

You should be interested in human behaviour and how to induce the desired conduct in a customer so that she or he will buy. Customers' backgrounds are different and therefore they have different values. One person will have been taught to make money work, to earn interest and profit, while another thinks of money simply as something to be spent as soon as possible. The basic background is the result of the way in which people have been living since their early childhood.

Attitudes

Attitudes are largely acquired and undergo changes, sometimes rapid changes. They are not as inflexible as those arising from backgrounds. If a person has been raised in a well-to-do home and has had a wide experience of the luxuries of life, this is not something that can undergo a rapid change. This is a factual background. That same person can, however, undergo substantial changes of attitudes during his or her life.

Customers act the way they do because of their basic backgrounds (which cannot readily be changed) and their attitudes (which have been acquired and are constantly being modified).

Conditions

In addition, there is the condition of the person at any one time.

80 RETAIL SELLING

These conditions are usually one or more of the following:

- Physical factors such as temperature of the room, illumination and ventilation.
- Organic factors such as hunger, fatigue, tiredness and anxiety.
- Specific factors such as those caused by alcohol, smoking and medicine.
- Abstract factors caused by such things as praise, reward, reproof and punishment.

The woman who has just returned from holiday is unlikely to want to talk about holiday-wear. The newly-married woman is quite a different person from the carefree girl she was a month or two ago. A customer who has had a poor night's sleep will react differently from his or her normal character.

People tend to be unpredictable and this gives rise to a real need for you to study your customers carefully when making sales presentations, because you must endeavour to find out their buying motives. Let us consider some of the more usual motives.

Physical pleasure

People like to give themselves pleasure and will respond to a sales talk about the ease of changing channels on their television with a remote control system; the 'cruise' control on a motor car; the easy movement from one program to another on a computer; the warmth of a winter coat; the lightness of a summer dress; the warmth and lightness of a duvet for a bed; the comfort and support of a chair; the comfort of a firm mattress, and so on.

By carefully observing the prospective customer—dress, mannerisms, accessories etc—and by adding suitable questions, you can decide whether pleasure is an important buying motive for the product being discussed.

The following short dialogue was overhead in a large department store that sells domestic appliances. The saleswoman had obviously decided that the customer wanted to enjoy herself.

Saleswoman: (Demonstrating an ice cream maker) It's simplicity itself. The container with the ice cream is removable so you don't have a problem when washing it. Simply take it out like this.

Customer:	That's novel.
Saleswoman:	Yes. It's the only model with a removable container. And there are so many recipes. Not just for ice cream, but for starters as well. Just look at these suggestions in the recipe book. (Showing book) I've done this one myself: iced avocado mousse. It's delicious as a starter, especially in the summer.

Relaxation and play

Manufacturers have not been slow in producing a whole range of electronic games and puzzles for use with or without our TV sets. Also, there has been a great increase in casual clothes and sportswear, because we tend to spend more and more time relaxing and on recreation at home and out-of-doors.

People are working fewer hours each week and finding that they have more time for leisure and relaxation. Acquiring things for pleasure and play has become a very powerful buying motive. It is not unusual for the whole family to visit a store when something substantial, such as a large tent or camping equipment, is being purchased.

Self-esteem and pride

We all like to feel important. This is why you must never give the slightest indication that you feel indifferent about a customer. You may feel 'under the weather', off-colour, depressed, or have had a poor night. You must not inflict these feelings on your customer and treat them indifferently.

If you have detected that a customer is thinking of buying a product to bolster his or her self-esteem, you will need to choose your words carefully. You cannot say outright that the product will give the customer status. You have to imply this obliquely.

Imitation

Imitation is a very strong buying motive. Think how many people follow fashion because of imitation. If a leading fashion designer has a show with short skirts and women start to wear short skirts, it cannot be because of universal, independent judgement by those women. It can only be because of the imitative motive.

Note how men change the width of their ties, the cut of their collars, the width of their trouser bottoms, the length of their hair. This is the motive of imitation, although it may be hard to get the men to acknowledge it.

Desire to be admired

Few people will admit that they wish to be admired, and by the opposite sex. Yet, this is why they wear certain clothes or sport certain styles. You must learn to recognize this motive, especially when your customer claims another reason for buying. Remember that there are at least two reasons why we do anything—a good reason and the *real* reason!

A customer might say 'It looks rather expensive, doesn't it?' or 'I think it looks rather smart' or even 'It looks simple yet elegant', indicating a tendency toward pride and self-esteem. Less pointed comments might be, 'What a pleasant colour', or 'There's quite a sheen on this as you turn it in the light.' Such comments would indicate that the customer should be sold on self-esteem and their desire to possess beautiful things.

Our needs

Very few things are bought for sheer necessity. Different products are bought for different reasons. Why do we buy a new pair of shoes? Because we have none at home?

Most of the things we purchase are not necessities; they are non-essentials and luxuries. If you give a poor sales presentation, the customer may have a change of mind and find reasons for not purchasing at that time.

Think of an occasion when you decided to buy something and, perhaps, were delayed in getting to the shop. By the time you arrived, the shop was closed for the day. The following day you were too busy and, when next you had the opportunity, your desire to buy that product had cooled considerably. In fact, there may even have been something else you wanted more by then!

BUYING MOTIVES AND SELLING POINTS

Forget your motives!

Continually search for the reasons that customers have for a purchase so that you can marshall the selling points of the product and relate them to the buying motives. Don't confuse your motives with those of the customer!

A simple example illustrates this: you may have a special line on which the store is making a larger-than-average profit and for which you may be receiving a higher-than-average commission (assuming that you have a commission scheme). As far as you are concerned, this would certainly be a selling point, but it would not be a customer benefit. A selling point, as we have suggested, is more aptly called a buying point: it is a plus-point why the customer should buy. A customer benefit is the advantage that the buyer or user will get from it.

Where to obtain product information

Manufacturers' literature and publicity on the products you are selling will provide you with a lot of information. You will gradually build up a large store of knowledge that can be put to good use as points to relate to a customer's buying motives. Your most telling points will be facts. If you are selling a 'non-stick' saucepan, make sure you can describe its properties from what you have learned from the manufacturer's literature.

If the customer asks you about the exotic fresh fruit you have on display, ensure that you know where they were grown. If the customer is not sure about the high quality of the hardwood in the furniture you are selling, be capable of explaining what it is, where it is grown, how it is seasoned and why it will not distort.

When a customer appears to rate the length of wear as important, you must be able to explain the hard-wearing qualities of the particular fabric. You can point to the strength and closeness of the weave. If you are asked how the garment is to be cleaned then stress how the manufacturer recommends the garment should be cleaned. Sometimes this is on a label attached to the product. Make sure you know the meanings of the symbols regarding washing, cleaning and ironing instructions on labels.

If the product is, say, a cardigan and you are wearing one, you could say, 'I've had this for over a year (or whatever it is) and it washes exceptionally well. It keeps its shape too.' Of course, you must never tell untruths, but you can often introduce your own personal experiences into your sales presentations if these are appropriate to the customer. In this way, it is possible to transmit a strong feeling of sincerity. On the other hand, insincerity is also very quickly passed on to the customer, so you must avoid making statements that are not your true beliefs.

Beware of equating your own lifestyle with that of the customer and making comments about what you do. This assumes that what you do must be good for the customer.

> 'I always drink this table wine.' (The customer may have entirely different tastes!)
> 'I find this product quite satisfactory.' (Why should the customer also be satisfied?)
> 'I've been using this cheap product for years.' (The customer might want to buy one for a gift)
> 'All my friends find these perfectly adequate.' (The customer is not one of your friends!)

Avoid using such comparisons as these unless they are right for the customer.

8
Test Closing

Test continually

As soon as the customer is satisfied that the product or merchandise is what is needed, you may assume that the customer is ready to buy. You cannot be sure just when the customer is prepared to buy, so you must test from time to time to see if that moment has arrived. Test closing means that if you do not sell at that point, you can continue with the sales presentation.

Test closing is also known as trial closing. If you close a sale with a trial close, it is no longer a test: you make a sale! If you watch a man working with a piece of wood that he is fitting to something, he might be planing and smoothing it, making it slightly smaller. Every so often, he tries it against the object he is working on and, if it is still too large, he continues with his smoothing down operation.

A woman knitting a pair of socks or a cardigan will pause from time to time when she has knitted a further length and measure it or place it against the person for whom it is being knitted. If it is not long enough, she carries on knitting.

At a football match you often hear the crowd shout, 'shoot!' because they think that the player with the ball should try to score a goal from that position at that moment.

If you are baking a cake, after an elapse of time, you open the oven carefully and insert a warm skewer in it to see if it emerges cleanly. If so, it is cooked; if not, the cake is put back into the oven, sometimes on a different shelf or with the heat adjusted, and left to cook for a further period of time.

Salesman: (After making his presentation and answering points raised by the customer) I'm sure you'll be more than happy with it. (Test closing) How would you like to pay, sir?

If the customer does not buy at this point, he may voice his reasons, or require another question to be answered, and the salesman can continue with the presentation.

Saleswoman: (After showing the merchandise, demonstrating how it operates and dealing with the customer's questions, tries test closing) Do you want the box or shall I wrap it separately?

Again, if the customer is not absolutely ready to buy, the sales presentation has not been ended.

If the customer is not ready to buy

There are many situations in which you test to see if things are ready; if not, you carry on until they are. Test, or trial, closing means just that. You think that you have sold the customer sufficiently so you 'have a go' to see if the customer will buy at that point.

If not, you carry on selling. This is the value of test closing. It is a test or trial at a particular point and, if the customer is still undecided, you will be asked other questions or be given expression of doubts. This means that the customer is not yet convinced that the sales proposition is the right one and is not ready to buy.

Fear of making a wrong purchase

We mentioned fear as the one big reason why people do not readily buy. Fear of making the wrong decision, fear of buying the wrong merchandise, fear that the product might not come up to expectations. If you try to close and the customer does not buy at that point you may not have allayed these fears sufficiently. You may have been too quick with your presentation, you may have rushed the customer; you may not have been sincere enough in your choice of phrases; you may not have communicated sufficiently clearly; you may not have covered the customer benefits adequately.

Test closing is similar to sticking the skewer into the cake to see if it is cooked. You go for the close to see if the customer is 'warm' enough to buy. You have to raise the temperature of desire enough for the customers to be convinced of the value of the product in terms of what it will do for them.

Knowing when to close

Opening a sale is not too difficult, although it requires practice; presentation is fairly straightforward; but knowing when to close is difficult. Although you know when to open and when to develop your presentation, you don't always know when it's time to try to close the sale. This is not just your problem; we all have the same difficulty.

We think we know when the 'right' moment has come but we are never sure until we have a go! Experienced sales people will tell you that they are never completely sure when a customer is ready to buy. Thus, you can see the value of testing. What you must ensure when you go for a trial close is that your lines of communication are kept open, because, if the customer will not close at that point, you must keep selling!

Obvious buying signs

Occasionally there are signs that will tell you that the time has arrived to close. A customer pulls out his cheque book; a woman takes her purse from her handbag. But these are obvious signs. We have to be very observant for those less obvious signs that tell us stage six has arrived: 'I should like to accept the offer because I approve the proposition that is being made to me.' Here are some for which you should be on the look-out:

A nod of the head

Watch people watching television. If they are concentrating on the transmission, they will often nod their heads in agreement with what is being said. If they disagree, they purse their lips and frown. Similarly, a customer will sometimes nod the head in agreement. This is an involuntary movement to oneself; it is giving approval to oneself. It is a sign for you to go for a test close.

A sparkle in the eye

Eyes don't really sparkle; they reflect light. Thus, when the eyes are opened wide, they give the impression of sparkling. Customers who have reached a decision and are ready to buy often open their eyes in this way. Sometimes it is accompanied by a slight smile or the raising of the eyebrows. Watch for this because it is often the sign, unconsciously made, that the time to close has arrived.

Watch all your customers when they reach the point of buying and you will learn the meanings of various facial expressions and body language.

Watch people looking at television and note how they experience emotions resulting from what they are watching. Watch people reading newspapers and see if there is any reaction to the articles they are reading.

Tone of the voice

When a customer approaches you and you start the sales presentation, the tone of the customer's voice is often different from the tone towards the end of the sale. Listen carefully for an alteration in this tone. It is usually upwards as the customer gets more excited inwardly.

Compare this with the commentaries you hear when a horse-race is approaching the finishing post. The commentator's voice rises higher and higher as the race nears its climax. Inward excitement takes charge of his voice. Listen carefully to your customers in future to hear if you can detect a change in the tone of the voice. When you do, it is time to go for a close.

Hesitation

When your customer hesitates, it may be the time to consider test closing. Hesitation signifies interest, but the customer may be hesitating for two different reasons. Hesitating whether to say 'yes'; hesitating whether to say 'no'. You will not know in which direction the hesitation is pointing. If you jump straight in and attempt to close brusquely, you could easily reinforce the hesitation and give the customer second thoughts. On the other hand, you could just as easily remove the hesitation and satisfactorily close the sale. What is the answer?

The best way is to attune yourself to the customer. To hesitate is to show interest and yet not to be convinced enough to buy. Agree with this by your actions and words. Go so far as to say, 'I'd rather you didn't buy it if you are not completely sure.' Hesitation means interest. The customer wants to be helped at this stage.

Hesitation and silence

The customer who hesitates is not sure; she or he is still thinking about it. Generally, your best response is silence. Say nothing, but listen.

If a woman is hesitating and she has a companion, note how often she turns to her companion and asks, 'What do you think?' When you have a customer who hesitates, don't press the point; pause, and listen. It may be necessary for you to help the customer by bringing out into the open the reasons for the indecision, but you can only do this if you pause, say nothing, and listen.

From here you may often find that you can go on to close because, as we have already said, hesitation means interest. If you bring the reasons out into the open, the chances are that 50 per cent of the time the hesitation will mean that the customer wishes to say 'yes'.

Value of test closing

You can appreciate the value of test closing. With hesitation apparent, it would be folly to attempt to close finally with the impression that if 'no' is said, then that is the end of it. Mostly customers want help in saying 'yes' to a sales proposition.

From the moment a customer faces you, you should be aiming to close the sale. Therefore test closing is not tried just once, but several times. If there is an underlying secret, it is: make it easy to buy.

There's no doubt about this: if you make it easy to buy, it's sure easier to sell!

Closing starts with the opening!

Closing starts at the beginning of the sales presentation. It is the result of an ordered presentation that begins as soon as you and the customer are face to face. Test close frequently, whenever you think the time may be right.

Some people know exactly what they want and will buy quickly. They don't need a full sales presentation; they don't want a long discussion. They know what it is they need and expect the sales assistant to complete the transaction quickly.

But there are many people who regard shopping as a social event. They like to visit various shops, mingle with other shoppers and look at the displays and offers. They do not always talk to sales people because they are not 'in the market' at that time.

You will need to distinguish between customers who merely want information and are obviously not going to buy there and then, and those who you suspect might purchase given the right conditions.

The customer is likely to buy at any point

At any moment in the sales presentation, the customer might be prepared to buy. Therefore ask leading questions such as:

- Do you prefer the teak or the oak finish?
- Which is the best day for us to deliver?
- Will you have removed the old ones before we deliver these?
- Do you want both, or just the one?
- We can easily shorten it; or would you prefer to do it yourself?

Watch for reactions, especially favourable ones. As soon as you detect a reaction you think is favourable, try for a close. If you find that the customer is not ready to buy, keep on selling.

From the start of the interview, keep test closing in mind by testing with questions. Don't over-complicate buying. Make it easy for the customer to understand. Test questions should spring from the assumption that the customer intends to buy. If you make this assumption from the start of the interview with the customer to the final test closing, you will avoid asking questions that raise doubts in the customer's mind. Your testing with questions is to see how far you are along the road towards a close.

Test closing a pen sale

Customer: I'd like to see some pens—or perhaps a pen and pencil set.

Saleswoman: Yes, sir. Do you have anything particular in mind?

Customer: Well. It's for my daughter. For her twenty-first birthday. I'd like to spend about £25.

Saleswoman: Here's a nice pen. (Shows one) A Parker with a gold nib. Does she like a fine or medium nib do you know? (Assuming that the customer is going to buy)

The saleswoman has selling points that are good buying points but she prefers to make them when more appropriate.

Customer: I'm not sure. She's at the university here. Does a lot of writing—I know that!

Saleswoman: Well, this one...

Customer: What about this one here? (Points into the display case)

Saleswoman: Ah! That's one of Sheaffer's more expensive models. It's £85 for the pen. (Not missing the opportunity of selling up) Here is the matching pencil. That's £65. It's really a beautiful set.

Customer: (Turning back to the original pen) How much would this set be?

Saleswoman: (Realizes that he intends to spend only about £25 and carefully presents something that is less than the customer's real desire) That is a very nice set. It's in stainless steel with a stainless steel nib. The set, pen and pencil, is £12. But, if it's for a twenty-first, I would suggest this set. I think it's more comfortable to hold than the stainless steel. It's one of Parker's special plastics. The set is £28. Gold nib and (making the sales point held in reserve) if she doesn't like the nib we can change it without any extra charge of course. She would really need to call in though. Would she be able to do that? (Going for a test close)

Customer: Oh, yes! Is there a case for it?
Saleswoman: (Knowing the sale is made and closing with an alternative) Yes, a very handsome case. (Showing case) As you can see it makes a splendid presentation gift. Now would you prefer this black case or this leather grained one?

Notice that the saleswoman started test closing almost as soon as the customer expressed his preference. (Incidentally, these sales dialogues are not fictitious. This particular one was overheard by the author while waiting for his own pen in a well-known shop in Oxford.)

With careful and natural questions the saleswoman has determined not only the nature of the gift but also the relationship between the customer and the recipient of the gift. When people make gifts they unconsciously wish to be judged by the size and value of the gift.

What exactly is the customer buying?

Little gifts that one gives to the person who has carried out the occasional service are usually quite different in value and prestige from those given as a result of many years' service, and different again from a present given to mark an anniversary.

People want to be known for the gifts they give. When, say, wedding gifts are being purchased, it is often important to know the approximate size and value of other people's gifts so that one can select one's own gift in the 'right' category: not too small and not too ostentatious.

Customer: It's actually for my niece who is getting married.
Salesman: (Realizing that this sale must be more than just a pair of pillow cases. Looks at the customer again and tries to decide whether she might pay a lot of money for the gift or not. He is unable to tell from his observation because the woman is moderately dressed, without jewellery, has a good leather handbag, well-kept hands, no make-up, speaks without an accent. He concludes that cost is not so

	important as quality but that the gift must be elegant and not flashy. He realizes that he may be completely wrong because he doesn't know anything about the niece) Is your niece young—I mean, would she appreciate something perhaps less traditional?
Customer:	Oh, yes! Quite young. Sensible though. I thought a pair of blankets might be acceptable.
Salesman:	(Ignores the suggestion but uses it to open his sales presentation) Well, the reason I asked you how old she is, is because I wondered whether she would appreciate a down duvet.
Customer:	Ah! I've heard of these but I know little about them. We don't have one.
Salesman:	Will you come and have a look? We have some on beds over here. (Takes customer to display section) Here is the double bed size. Put your hand underneath. (Customer does so) Can you feel the heat? It builds up from the heat of your hand.
Customer:	Goodness me! That is remarkable. What is it?

The customer is interested and the salesman will continue with his presentation assuming all the while that the customer intends to purchase.

With many sales you can use leading questions like these, but, to be effective, you must always listen carefully to the answers.

Open and closed questions

As a professional sales person in your field, you will possess much more knowledge than many customers whom you serve. Therefore, in dealing with these customers, you must be able to control the selling process. This can best be done by the use of two sorts of questions:

- Closed questions
- Open probes

A closed question is one that obtains specific answers such as 'yes', 'no' 'black', 'white', 'three', 'sixteen', etc. Such questions are usually in the form of 'How many?' 'How often?' 'How much?' Examples of closed questions are:

- How many rooms do you have that need attention?
- How many metres do you need?
- How often do you want the boiler on during the day?
- How many gallons do you use each time?
- How much would you want to make at any one time?
- Do you have AC or DC equipment?
- Do you want wool or cotton?
- Will you be using this in your car?
- Do you want to take this overseas?
- Do you have travel insurance?
- Will you want single or double beds?
- Shall we put this on account?
- Can I book your order now?
- May I make out the invoice now?
- You have sufficient to complete the job?

All these questions are closed questions endeavouring to obtain answers that will narrow down the conversation into specific directions. Closed questions are most important for controlling the selling process, especially towards the close.

Open probes

Open probes ask for more information. They invite the customer to expand on the subject. They cannot usually be answered by a single response and are the opposite of closed questions. Consider the following opposites:

Closed	*Open*
Would you like it in pink or blue?	What shade were you thinking of? You have mainly pink in the other rooms. What do you think about this one?
Will you take eight, or the pack of ten?	How many cartons might you need now and if you tackle the same job later on? How can you use these again?

(closed continued)	(open continued)
	What if you don't have enough?
Are you getting poor reproduction because the stylus is worn?	Why is that, do you think? Oh! Hm! I suppose you've had it for some time. How often does this happen? I see. (Stays silent)

Narrow down or open up conversation

You don't have to think too much about whether you are going to use a closed question or an open probe. It is the reason behind its use that you consider.

You either want to narrow down the presentation to move it to a satisfactory close, or you need more information. Open probes explore the general areas of a customer's needs; closed questions get to the core.

The use of the pronoun 'we' instead of 'you' automatically includes you in the customer's quest. Whenever appropriate, instead of asking, 'What size are you looking for?' use 'What size are we looking for?' It puts you on the same side; both of you are searching for answers to the customer's problems.

9
Working for Repeats

Customer satisfaction

Customers who are satisfied with your products and the manner in which you serve them will be willing to return and buy other things from you. If repeat purchases are not appropriate for them, they will tell their friends and colleagues of the standard of service they received.

Keep this repeat sales business in mind when you serve customers. It will have an effect on all your presentations and help you to make repeat sales, if not to the same customer, to that customer's acquaintances.

Frequency of purchase

A large proportion of your customers may be strangers and unlikely to return repeatedly to make other purchases. On the other hand, if you are selling foodstuffs, you will tend to see them regularly every few days or every week.

If you are selling television sets, furniture, kitchenware, carpets, clothes, curtains or typewriters, you are selling infrequently purchased items. Working for repeat sales doesn't seem to apply in your case. But you still can't afford to forget the repeat sales factor: your customers will talk about you and your store to other people and thus convey good (or poor) impressions.

For example, you may have pleased a customer by the way you treated him, the extent to which you were prepared to go in helping him to choose the right goods and the trouble you took to ensure that delivery would be on the day he desired.

WORKING FOR REPEATS

Salesman: Good afternoon, sir.
Customer: Good afternoon. There's something in the window I'd like to see, please.
Salesman: Certainly, sir. What is it?
Customer: It's a fan. There are two but it's the smaller I'd like to see.
Salesman: Oh, yes! Those are the last two I have until fresh stock arrives. This hot weather has nearly cleaned me out. (Leaves the counter and goes to the window and, after a pause, returns with a small electric fan which he places on the counter)
Customer: Ah! That's it. How much is it?
Salesman: (Looking at the ticket on the fan) £26. That includes VAT.
Customer: Hmm!
Salesman: I'll just plug it in and show you. (Does so)
Customer: Hmm! That's fine.
Salesman: Yes. As I said, this is one of the last two. Do you have a large area you wish to cool?
Customer: Not really. It's my study and it gets a lot of sun. When it's hot like this, if I open the window it doesn't help.
Salesman: Well, this fan is suitable for a small room and should certainly make you feel more civilised.
Customer: (Putting his hand to his face) And the other one; the larger one.
Salesman: That's an oscillating fan; As you say it's a little larger.
Customer: I think I'll have this one but—er—could I see the other?
Salesman: Certainly. Just a moment. (Goes to window again and brings back the larger fan) Here you are.
Customer: Oh yes! It is bigger, isn't it. I'm sorry. But er—
Salesman: No problem, sir. While it's out, I'll show you it working. (Removes the connection from the small fan and connects it to the larger one)
Customer: Oh! I say. It's much more powerful.

98 RETAIL SELLING

Salesman: Yes, but you are near to it. You wouldn't want a fan to be this near to where you're sitting. Ideally, it should be placed in a corner of the room and directed upward. That way, you get a good circulation of cooled air without a draught.

Customer: And that's how much?

Salesman: (Looking at the ticket on the fan) That's £38. Tax paid, of course.

Customer: Hmm!

Salesman: (Selling up) Of course, the real value of this fan is that not only does it move a larger volume of air per minute, it oscillates like this (Adjusts fan which turns slowly from side to side)

Customer: (Interested) Hmm!

Salesman: You can also adjust it to oscillate on one side only like this. (Carries out necessary slight adjustment)

Customer: Hmm! Could I see the other one working again, please?

Salesman: Of course, sir. (Transfers electrical connection back to the smaller fan)

Customer: (Stands several feet away from the fan) I see what you mean about standing near to it. You can only just feel it back here.

Salesman: How large is the room in which you're going to use it?

Customer: Oh! I suppose about twelve or thirteen feet square. Well, it's not square; slightly 'L' shaped, but not large.

Salesman: Well, this small fan would be quite useful.

Customer: All right. I'll take it. £26, you say?

Salesman: Yes, sir.

Customer: I'll pay by cheque.

Salesman: Fine, sir. (Disconnects electric supply) Would you like the box?

Customer: No, thank you. It can go in my car. It's just outside.

Salesman: You have a year's unconditional guarantee with it. If anything goes wrong, bring it back. Although, touch wood, I haven't had any

	complaints with this make at all. (Brings invoice pad to counter and starts to write) May I have your name, sir?
Customer:	Jones—A M Jones.
Salesman:	Ah! Will you need a plug?
Customer:	Yes. Yes, please, I will.
Salesman:	Thirteen-amp fitting, is it, sir?
Customer:	Yes.
Salesman:	But you'll need a three-amp fuse. I'll just make sure this one is OK for you.
Customer:	Thank you.
Salesman:	(Continues writing on invoice pad)
Customer:	(Takes out cheque book and starts to write)
Salesman:	I have a rubber stamp for the name to save you. (Brings it to counter)
Customer:	You know—that oscillating fan certainly seems to have a greater advantage.
Salesman:	(Stops writing and looks up) Of course, sir. It's much more effective because not only does it move a greater volume of air, it can spread over the whole room.
Customer:	Hmm!
Salesman:	It oscillates through 90° so if it is placed in a corner it will cover the whole room left to right about every ten seconds. The smaller fan you're having, is in one direction only. And moves about two-thirds of the volume of air.
Customer:	(Obviously thinking) Hm!
Salesman:	(Says nothing but disconnects the small fan and reconnects the larger, oscillating fan) Perhaps you'd like to stand where you did before, sir, and feel the difference.
Customer:	(Stands in same spot as before and waits while the fan oscillates twice in his direction) You're right. It is more suitable for me. Would it be too much trouble to change and have it?
Salesman:	Not at all, sir. It's no trouble. If you're working in your study with the sun on the window, you'll get more benefit from this one. I didn't tell you just now because I thought you preferred the smaller one, but this one also has three speeds. So, when it is very hot,

100 RETAIL SELLING

	you use the highest speed by turning this knob here (demonstrates) and, when it is not so hot, you turn down to the lowest speed here. (Demonstrates)
Customer:	I see. In fact, a much better fan altogether.
Salesman:	Of course, sir. The motor is also larger and it's altogether a much more robust machine. You're paying another £12 but you're certainly getting more than that in value. This is the one we have in the rear office.
Customer:	Fine. Thank you. Thank you for being so helpful.
Salesman:	Not at all, sir. You need something that will do the job to your satisfaction. I'll just alter the invoice.

This man is unlikely to return in the near future to buy another fan. But it is almost a certainty that when he is asked by friends and relations where such a product can be obtained, this shop will be mentioned.

You will also be surprised at the number of times a customer will come back to repeat a purchase for a friend, or with a friend, simply because you have given good service and have acted the part of a real sales person.

A customer returns

We read earlier of a woman being helped to choose a wedding present for her niece and the salesman showing a genuine, sincere interest in her quest. After about a month, that same woman returned to the store and purchased two single duvets and covers for her own use. The sales actually took place at a department store in Camberley, Surrey, and were reported to the author by the salesman who was attending a management course on selling.

Do not regard each sale as a complete and separate operation but as part of a continuing process. You want customers to come back again and again to buy from you. If, during your sales presentation, no matter how long and difficult it may be, you act as though you would be pleased to see them again, you will be working for repeat business. You can detect the need for enthusiasm here.

Type of product and degree of repeat

Of course, a lot will depend on the type of merchandise you are selling. If you sell cigarettes, soap, newspapers, soft drinks, sweets, groceries, socks, shirts, vests, pants, woollens, etc you will find that customers tend to have a certain loyalty to you and return repeatedly to make other purchases.

This loyalty will be enhanced if you are interested in them enough to recall their names when they return to your store. This requires genuine enthusiasm for your job and is something you have to work at, as you will have read in Chapter 5. A famous American general wrote:

> You are as young as your faith,
> As old as your doubt,
> As young as your self-confidence,
> As old as your hope,
> As old as your despair.
> Years may wrinkle your skin, but,
> To give up enthusiasm wrinkles your soul.

Enthusiasm stimulates repeat business

As we keep stressing, enthusiasm is perhaps the most important characteristic you can possess in selling. Properly and sincerely expressed, it can bring you a lot of repeat business. As you now know, enthusiasm does not just happen: you have to work at it. And the best way to work at it is to consume knowledge. This includes knowledge about your goods, their uses and different applications; and knowledge about your customers, their needs, wants and desires.

Enthusiasm for repeat business means developing your knowledge of customers. If they only visit your store occasionally, it will be difficult. They will remember you, but you will find it difficult to remember all the people you serve. You might remember the face and perhaps even the previous occasion when the customer called, but it is impractical to try to put a name to most of them. It is the way in which you conduct the reunion that makes the customer feel at ease. Here are some of the ways you can welcome an 'old face'.

'Hullo, sir. Let me see—er—you bought the —'

'Hullo, madam. For the moment I can't recall your previous purchase—'
'Hullo, sir: I did serve you last time, didn't I.' (Statement)
'Good afternoon, sir. When were you in here last?'
'Good morning, madam (if you do remember her) how nice to see you again.'

The hallmark of a good sales person is knowledge, particularly knowledge of the customers. It becomes power when organized and directed into plans for action. It breeds enthusiasm. And enthusiasm is of great value in helping you to make repeat sales.

Enthusiasm is in oneself

Enthusiasm is the outward reflection of our inner self. It reflects our belief in ourselves, our store, our company, the products we sell and the service we give.

New man: (To a new colleague in a store he has just joined) What are the people like here?
Old hand: Why? What were they like at your other store?
New man: Oh! They were a miserable lot. I found them very difficult to get on with. They were always moaning and making life difficult.
Old hand: Hmm! I reckon you'll find them much about the same here!

The world without is a reflection of the world within. How we see the world and the way that people act is mostly the way we act ourselves. We have to think enthusiastically to be enthusiastic. In this way we affect other people who are then pleased to talk to us and do business with us.

Enthusiasm is infectious

Enthusiasm is infectious; it turns prospects into customers. If we are genuinely enthusiastic it enables customers to overcome their fears and doubts. Customers like being served by really enthusiastic sales people.

Saleswoman: (To customer) I was fortunate to be able to buy one of the first pairs that arrived. Oh! They're marvellous. I wouldn't be without them for the world.

There is no way that you can mistake this saleswoman's enthusiasm for the goods she has bought. Certainly, the customer will be impressed.

Salesman: (To customer he has served before) It's very nice to see you again, sir. I hadn't seen you for some time and wondered where you were.

Genuine enthusiasm will influence customers; one of the simplest ways to welcome a customer back is to say so. But it must be genuine. You must not welcome back someone you have never seen before.

At one restaurant I know, the head waiter often greets clients by saying, 'How nice to see you again, sir', even though the client has never been to the restaurant before. The restaurant has a good reputation for food, and may be described as expensive. The intention of the waiter is to make clients feel important, especially if they are with guests. The guests will think that their host is in the habit of eating at the restaurant.

However, this is a very doubtful ploy. If a man and his wife visit the restaurant for the first time to mark a special celebration, and the head waiter welcomes the man back as an old patron, the wife would be justified in expecting a suitable explanation! Pleas by the husband of 'I've never been here before!' might not placate the wife and the simple incident could well damage the celebration.

Saleswoman: (To customer) I know you'll be happy with them, madam. And later on we'll be having our autumn range. I've seen a few of the samples and they're super. Certainly there are some that will complement the ones you're buying now for spring. They've designed them so that you can wear a combination for those evenings when it's not warm and yet not cold enough for autumn clothes.

Salesman: (To customer buying a garden cultivator) To start with you won't need more than the basic machine and the plough attachment. You can add the automatic hoe as and when you feel like it. If you're planting potatoes or bulbs later on, you can add the planter; it plants and ridges at the same time. The makers have really given a lot of thought to the small nursery operation.

Salesman: (To customer) May I suggest, don't take the universal aerial now. You may not need it. I think you'll find that the set's powerful enough to work perfectly well without it. If you're going to use it in places where reception really is difficult, then you'll need the universal. There's no need to spend money you don't have to.

These are examples of enthusiastic sales people helping their customers to buy and, at the same time, working for repeat business. Repeat business is not necessarily returning to buy the same products; it is returning to the same store and, preferably, to you. This is what is meant by working for repeat business. Make yourself attractive to customers by the way in which you serve them and guide their purchases.

Knowledge plus enthusiasm work for repeats

Enthusiasm radiates the knowledge we have gained. It radiates this knowledge as a fire radiates heat and the customer becomes warmed to the proposition. Customers naturally like to be served by enthusiastic people who possess sufficient knowledge to answer their questions.

Enthusiasm ensures repeats. It is this plus-value in selling which makes all the difference between a mediocre sales person and a real sales person.

10
Selling Convincingly

How to avoid scepticism

Every time you make a strong claim for one of your products during a sales presentation, the chances are that the customer will be sceptical. The customer will give a look, raise an eyebrow, or even say something aloud. The stronger your claim, the greater the chance of disbelief.

> Salesman: Sir, you could walk 20 miles in these socks, without shoes, and you wouldn't wear a hole in them!

How can a customer possibly believe that! Supposing this were true, how would you convince the customer of the truth of the statement?

It's no use asking him to take a pair and try them out. Of course, you would only use such a strong claim if in fact it had been done. You should be able to show the customer proof with photographs, an extract from a paper, or the manufacturer's folder describing the reasons why the socks stand up to such use. In other words, you have to bring a reliable witness to testify for you. The greater the claim you are making, the stronger the witness you need.

Bring witnesses to support you

If you want to sell convincingly, always have a witness that you can offer in evidence.

> Customer: I see these tights are light, but are they strong?

106 RETAIL SELLING

Salesman: Here's a pair we use to show customers. (Takes hold of each end and pulls them apart until his arms are extended) Might this be strong enough, madam? They haven't torn anywhere.

Salesman: This article is completely non-flammable, sir.
Customer: Do you mean that if I put a match to it, it would not burn?

The salesman offers the article and a box of matches to the customer and invites him to try.

These are drastic demonstrations and it is unlikely that you will ever be required to demonstrate anything quite so dramatically. Nevertheless, the underlying principle is the same in any sales presentation.

When you make a claim for a product, introduce a witness to testify on behalf of what you are saying. Such witnesses may be a demonstration, manufacturer's literature, a newspaper cutting, letter from satisfied customers, a reference to other users, or whatever gives credence to your claims.

Customer: This coat is too light. I want a really warm one.
Salesman: Although it's light in weight, it is warmer than one double its weight. (Customer looks in disbelief. Salesman introduces a witness) Please try it on while I go and fetch a heavier one. There's a fitting room over there. I think you might be very surprised, sir.

The salesman does not contradict the customer. He does not say 'You are wrong'. He does not try to win an argument which, in fact, he could because of the extremely high thermal properties of the coat. He simply tells the customer that he might be surprised.

Customer: No! I don't think so. It's not strong enough.
Salesman: (Doesn't argue, doesn't contradict, doesn't say that it is strong enough, simply introduces a witness) If it will support this (pointing to an article in the store) would that be strong enough, sir?
Customer: Easily.
Salesman: (Demonstrates) There you are, sir. In fact, it will support more than twice that amount.

SELLING CONVINCINGLY

You cannot always convince a customer by words alone of claims you are making for a product. You must have support; you must have a witness. In the same way that the defendant in a court case who claims that he was somewhere else when the crime was committed has to have witnesses to corroborate his statement, you need witnesses to testify for your claims.

The best witness

Your witness must be convincing, and nothing could be more convincing to a customer than the customer's own experience. If you can get the customer to act as a witness for your claim, then little can stop you from selling. If you say that something is the softest material you have ever felt, get the customer to feel the product and agree with you.

If the products you are selling can be demonstrated, learn how to use them thoroughly. When using the demonstration as a witness, make sure that you have practised the routine so that the customer can follow you. Any confusion or mishandling you introduce at this stage adversely affects the customer's belief in what you have been saying.

You cannot overdo this technique of getting a witness for your claims. You may think that you are overdoing it, especially when you say the same thing to different customers day after day. It is amazing how often you have to say something to 'get it across' to a customer so that the customer really believes it. While the easiest method is to get the customer to try the product by feeling it, holding it, operating it, many cannot be demonstrated in this way.

Demonstrate products convincingly

Some products are difficult to demonstrate. It is difficult to demonstrate a heated food trolley; you cannot have it switched on with food in it for hours. Carpets piled together in a department look quite different from one set in a room in the customer's home. It's not easy to demonstrate products such as a blowtorch, firelighter or watering can in the store, nor can you always operate machinery and equipment.

Remember, however, we are looking for witnesses and we should only consider demonstrations insofar as they testify to our claims.

108   RETAIL SELLING

If you are going to show a product to prove what you have been saying, show the whole product and not just a part of it. If it is appropriate and possible, show the product in use.

A long-sleeve pullover should be taken out of its packaging, opened out and held up against your body so that the customer can see what it looks like before trying it on. Your department supervisor will tell you what can be removed from the manufacturer's original packagings and what cannot.

If you are selling ties, learn to wind a folded double thickness of the tie over and around the thumb to give the impression of a knotted tie. Place this against a shirt to give an even greater impression.

If you are unpacking a product from its box, learn how to do this quickly and quietly. Even more important, know exactly how to repack it in the box. The fact that you can do this with ease will impress the customer.

Develop dexterity in handling your products

If you are selling a fairly complicated piece of equipment, practise with that equipment on your own until you are skilled and accomplished at handling it. Know where everything is, what every knob, switch, lever, button, etc does. Don't wait until you have a customer in front of you before you read the maker's instructions to see how it works or how it switches on!

Create confidence with your customer

When you have established confidence between yourself and the customer you can say such things as 'One of my customers has had her so-and-so for over two years and it is still good as new.'

You will see that you have to cultivate a convincing manner. This is slightly different from what we have been saying so far. So far we have looked at the substance of a convincing sales presentation; now we need to look at the manner of the presentation.

How you say something is often more important than what you say. You can probably think of people you know who have mannerisms of speech and presentation that make it difficult for you to believe them. They don't sound convincing. To develop a convincing manner, here are some rules to follow:

Stand upright

Stand erect so that your posture is as upright as your speech. Don't lounge or lean against fixtures. If you must rest, sit down. Avoid irritating, meaningless body movements. Don't play with a pencil, ball-point or any other item.

Can you remember seeing someone being interviewed on television who is not used to talking in public? Can you remember how that person tended to fidget with his body, perhaps swaying from side to side, or backwards and forwards? Not only do such unnecessary movements of the body disturb the smooth flow of the sales presentation, they create mistrust.

We are all nervous at times

Of course, one has to make allowances for nervousness, but you will soon learn to get over your initial 'nerves'. When showing a customer a product, there is every reason why you should be definite with your body movements, especially with your hands when you are pointing out a feature to the customer. Don't wave them around in the air: it is not very convincing. Also be careful not to be forceful because this gives an impression of your being domineering, and your attempts to close might suffer.

Eye contact

Cultivate steady eye contact. Don't look over the customer's shoulder at some point in the rear. Check this effect; the next time you are with a friend look over his/her shoulder more than you look in the eyes. Before long your friend will be looking around and asking what is so interesting there!

You can easily create uneasiness if you do not look your customers in the eye. This does not mean you indulge in a staring match, because you must look from the customer to the product from time to time. Ignore any external happenings when you are making a sales presentation. Concentrate on eye contact by looking for the colour of the eyes and this will give you an advantage.

Speak clearly

Cultivate a steady voice. Speak clearly and do not gabble. Sound the endings of words. Take special care with the 'g' on the end of words such as clothing, bedding, sleeping, walking, and so on.

You are unlikely to have met the customer before; therefore, your appearance and voice will create an impression with the other person. Your voice is part of your personality and will create an image with your customers. To project a pleasing personality you must develop a pleasing, easy-to-understand voice and speech pattern.

Don't try to change your voice into some sort of Shakespearean orator. You are not going on the stage. You do not have to project your voice to the back of the hall. But you do have to transmit your messages so that your customer will understand you. You have to achieve the objective you have set for yourself; your voice is an important means of doing this.

No one can communicate

Your voice is your transmitting tool. Although you are in the communicating business, you cannot communicate on your own; you can only transmit. No one person can communicate; it takes at least two. Thus, when you speak to a person, you are carrying out only one part of the communications activity — transmitting.

Communicating with people is not always easy. People jump to conclusions, and frequently use private languages. But people understand simple words.

For effective communications the other person has to receive correctly what you transmit. Therefore you must ensure that your voice is in good condition and your speech is relevant to the listener.

Private languages

The problem becomes more acute when unusual words are used or when ordinary words are used with unusual meanings. You may think that such difficulties are easily avoided, but that's not always the case. In almost every trade, industry and profession there are special words or special meanings to common words.

SELLING CONVINCINGLY 111

All professions and businesses have their own vocabulary. In education there are a number of 'disciplines': these are different major subjects. In advertising you will hear someone comment on 'a nice piece of artwork' — well-formed letters and illustrations to be used for making an advertisement.

In the printing industry, which has perhaps one of the largest private languages, you will find that it is sometimes possible to 'bleed the edges but you can't bleed in the gutter'; that you 'can get more copy if you use a lower case'; that 'off-set' and 'set-off' are two entirely different things.

There is nothing wrong with a private language. Its use is essential in the particular industry for intelligent communications to take place. Such language has grown out of the developments and peculiarities in those industries. Some of your customers will often use a private language. You must be aware of this tendency and learn to use it correctly with those customers. Equally, you must be aware of your jargon and abbreviations that may be misunderstood by your customers.

Work on the principle that if it is possible that your words can be misunderstood, they will be.

Use simple words

People understand simple words, but you cannot always confine your speech to words of one syllable. Certainly it is undesirable that you should. You should learn to use words correctly and mix long words with lots of short ones. However, remember that short, simple words create effective messages.

Cultivate three rules:

- Use simple words with simple meanings.
- Use words that you know are familiar to the customer.
- Make statements that can have only one meaning.

Breathe in before you speak

Make sure you have enough breath before you start talking and avoid breaking up your sentences into three and four word groups because you haven't taken enough air into your lungs.

If you are going on a car journey, you make sure you have

sufficient fuel in the tank. If you wish to water the garden, you will know whether you have collected sufficient rainwater. If you intend to paint a door, you will need a certain amount of paint. If you try to blow out all the candles on your birthday cake, you will need to store a certain amount of puff before you blow!

If you are going to sell convincingly to a customer, you must transmit your messages in succinct, controllable passages. You need enough breath to do this. You must control your breath, and control your speech.

Breathe properly

It is only when we exert ourselves that we become aware of breathing. Run up a hill, play tennis, play with the dog, run for a train, and you are aware of your breathing. When we are doing our normal work, we are not aware of how many times a minute we are using our lungs—in slowly, out slowly.

If you are going to start breathing deeply, sit down. If you stand up while you do it, you are likely to feel dizzy because the lungs are not used to taking in a lot of air unless the body needs it for some particular exertion. A good exercise is to see how far you can read aloud from a passage with only one breath.

This does not mean you struggle on and on gasping to get the last few words out. It means that you take a reasonably deep breath and read aloud to see how far you get while the words are still comfortably within your control, and you still have air left in the lungs.

Sit in a firm chair, take a moderate breath, breathe out—pause—breathe in again moderately, then read a passage aloud and see how far you get with just the one breath.

Most important word

The most important word you will speak to a prospect is his or her name. Some names, of course, are a little difficult to pronounce. Never be afraid of asking how a name is spelled. When you know it, use it in your conversation.

You will have appreciated now that articulating words, that is, making the mouth and tongue work correctly so that the words mean something, is vitally important to you. Do not indulge in 'slurvian' — slovenly speech. Here is an exercise in slurvian: what do you think the following mean? (Answers are at the end of the chapter.)

1. Lor
2. Lore
3. Bean
4. Plight
5. Sport
6. Fiscal
7. Par
8. War
9. Goh-i
10. Itinry

Give every syllable its true value. Make sure you sound the 't' in words such as water, butter, better. A number of people suppress the sound of 't' in their speech. This practice is called the glottal stop. It is cutting off air and throttling the 't' in the throat.

Avoid placing the sound of the letter 'l' on the ends of words such as 'idea', unless you really want to say 'ideal'. Make sure that any word that ends in 'ing' doesn't sound as though it ends in 'in'.

It is not only what you say to prospects but how you say it. And how you say it means the sound, pitch and generally how you articulate.

Slovenly English is as sloppy as having part of your previous meal strewn on your tie or dress.

If you have the opportunity of listening to yourself on a tape recorder, do so. Say 'Good morning, madam' into the machine. You might be surprised to find that the 'd' is lost from 'good', or the 'g' from 'morning'.

Accents and dialects

Apart from speaking clearly, do not worry about accents in the slightest, except where accents are confused with dialects. Do not use dialect; in a professional environment, it should be avoided.

'Um—er! Well—y' know!'

Avoid too many 'ums' and 'ers'. When next you are shopping listen carefully to the assistants. Count how many 'ums' and 'ers' you hear! Yet another defect in speaking is to start every sentence with the world 'well'. People unaccustomed to being interviewed on radio and TV often start answers to questions with the word, 'well', and then interject into all their answers the needless 'y' know'!

114 RETAIL SELLING

Customer: Do you stock umbrellas, please?
Salesman: Well—um—y' know—we used to.
Customer: Do you stock them now?
Salesman: Well—as I said we used to—and um—let me see if—er—what kind are you looking for, sir?
Customer: Dammit! (Irritated) One to keep the rain off!
Salesman: Ha! Ha! Well—um—shall I go and...
Customer: Look, don't bother. I'll try next door in the butchers!

If you want to sell convincingly, cultivate a steady voice and take care to give every syllable its proper stress and remove all those irritating 'ums' and 'ers'. When in doubt consult a good dictionary.

Help the customer to buy

Finally, to be convincing and to sell convincingly, cultivate the habit of helping the customer to buy. Don't swamp the customer in a torrent of words; ask questions that show a genuine interest in the customer's needs; listen to the answers. Imagine the following conversation with your doctor.

You: I feel terrible, doctor. I have a pain in my neck and down my back.
Doctor: Hmm! Pain, eh. Now what you need are some aspirins. I'll give you enough to last you for two or three days. Come back and see me if it doesn't clear up.

Doctors do not act like this, of course, but you can imagine what little confidence you would after such a consultation.

The customer buys a suit

Sales assistants sometimes fail to transmit confidence to their prospective customers. The salesman in the following dialogue creates confidence by helping the customer to buy.

Customer: I'd like to see some of your lightweight suits, please.
Salesman: I take it you'd like ready-made, sir?

SELLING CONVINCINGLY

Customer: Yes, please
Salesman: May I just run the tape round your chest?
Customer: I'm a 42.
Salesman: Very well, sir. I'll get a 42. A 42 regular I think, sir. (Selects a suit sized 42 as requested by the customer although with ready-mades, especially lightweights, he knows that it is better to measure than to go by manufacturers' sizes) Can we just try the jacket on for size?
Customer: (Looking in the mirror) That looks quite nice.
Salesman: Yes, sir. I wonder if it's a little on the short side. (Genuinely concerned that the jacket is too short)
Customer: You think so?
Salesman: I think I'd like to try on a longer fitting. Just a moment, sir (Fetches a different size) Will you try this please, sir.
Customer: Hmm! That's even better.
Salesman: I think we should try the trousers on for an overall impression.
Customer: Of course. Where's the—um?
Salesman: (Indicating the fitting room) Over there, sir.
Customer: (Eventually emerges from the fitting room) I think this looks quite well.
Salesman: Yes, sir. I'm not sure whether the trousers need to be shortened slightly. Do you like them just breaking on the shoes?

There is no need to go on with this interview because the point is made: the salesman is helping the customer to buy. In fact, he is selling.

You must cultivate the habit of helping the customer to buy. By doing so, you will be selling convincingly. Present your sales case strongly. Try for a close when you think that it is the right time to conclude the sale. Answer any objections boldly but confidently in a relaxed manner, and regard the customer as far more important than just the one sale.

116 RETAIL SELLING

Answers to exercise

1. Law. Often badly spoken, especially when used in 'lore and order'
2. Lower. Two syllables.
3. Being. Again, there are two syllables.
4. Polite. The 'o' often gets lost in the mouth.
5. Support. The stress is incorrectly placed on the second syllable.
6. Physical. This is just laziness; it has three syllables.
7. Power. A somewhat affected way of saying it.
8. Water. Often pronounced 'wa-er'.
9. Got it? Often pronounced with the glottal stop.
10. Itinerary. This has five syllables — i-tin-er-ra-ry. Most people seem to settle for four, or even three!

Case Study: Nelson's Store

John Nelson is probably the most aggressive retailer in Bath. Although his electrical store is not the largest in town, it is likely that his profits exceed those of a comparably sized store anywhere in the city. Through effective stock control he has been able to achieve a high turnover, high stock-turn, and an unusually high mark-up. He maintains a good range of stock and displays it to give the impression of a very wide assortment.

There are a number of electrical stores in this south-western English city of some 80,000 inhabitants. Two of the stores are very exclusive and handle such things as very expensive hi-fi equipment; several in the outlying districts cater for the lower and lower-middle class of trade. Nelson's and one or two others cater for the middle and upper end of the trade.

Nelson's began as a lower-middle class store and also catered for the local handymen. After several years it moved to premises nearer to the centre of Bath, close to Milsom Street, the fashionable shopping street, and not far from large stores such as Marks & Spencer.

Despite the fact that Bath is not an industrialized city, a large proportion of the inhabitants work in the industrial complexes between Bath and Bristol. Nelson had always enjoyed a high customer loyalty from this group of people and was a little concerned about his present image.

To obtain information on several problems that bothered him he commissioned a research company to undertake a customer analysis. His main problems were:

SELLING CONVINCINGLY

- Should he take steps to clarify the image of his store?
- What image should he seek to convey?
- Are his prices too high for the market he is trying to reach?

Personal interviews were conducted among 250 customers chosen at random on Tuesday, Wednesdays, Thursdays, Fridays and Saturday mornings. Fifty-eight per cent of those interviewed were men; 42 per cent were women. The number of those interviewed who had purchased was 48 per cent; nonpurchasers were 52 per cent. The main findings were:

Respondents' Classification of Nelson's

High prices	13.6% of total responses
Above average prices	45.0
Average prices	36.0
Low prices	0
No response	5.4

Atmosphere in Store

Exclusive	29.6%
Average to exclusive	34.0
Average	30.7
Below average	0
No response	5.7

What respondents liked about Nelson's

Quality merchandise	24.0%
Past satisfaction	3.0
Wide selection	24.0
Good brand names	8.0
Fair prices	2.0
Outstanding service	19.0
Excellent sales personnel	48.0

What respondents did not like about Nelson's

Lack of adequate parking facilities	4.2%
Limited selection of products	3.6
Too high prices	1.6
Low quality products	8.9
Staff not well-informed	4.4

All the comments were suggested independently by the respondents in answer to open-ended questions.

1. Did the survey provide the information needed by John Nelson?
2. What changes should be made in his operation as a result of this survey?

11
Sales Policy versus Profit Policy

Sales policy

Sales policy concentrates on how to sell products to customers. It includes the selling activity, displays, promotion, advertising, demonstrations, special price offers, and anything else that helps to sell the products.

The emphasis is on sales volume. The more we sell, the greater the turnover; the greater the turnover, the higher the profit.

If we receive a commission on the products we sell, the more we sell, the more commission we receive. It is understandable that everyone is interested in sales.

Inside the store, we make no money. Everything you see in the store costs money. The stock, fittings, people's wages, displays, advertising, staff canteen, lighting and power all cost money. It is only when a customer walks through the door and offers to buy some of our products that we have the opportunity to sell something and make a profit.

Profit

The difference between the cost of our products and what they are sold for is profit. But it's not what we think of as pure profit; it is gross profit. We call it gross profit because from it we have to deduct a proportion towards paying for all those costs we mentioned above, fittings, wages, displays, etc. And, of course, your commission.

Stores do not buy single products; they buy in quantities. The quantities they purchase will depend on the size of the product, how much space they will occupy, how much they cost and how

SALES POLICY VERSUS PROFIT POLICY

quickly they can be sold. You can appreciate one of the buyer's problems: a sufficient quantity must be purchased to satisfy likely customer demand, but not so much that it remains unsold. Products must not be kept in stock too long because they go out of fashion, are superseded by an improved model, or deteriorate.

There is also the fact that it costs money to keep products in stock; this experience includes the actual cost of the goods and the cost of stocking them.

Some products, such as fresh fish, have to be sold very quickly; others, such as greengroceries, have a life of a few days. Ordinary groceries have a month or more; clothing, six to nine months. At the other end of the scale, jewellery, expensive watches, silver cutlery, and similar items, can stay in stock for up to two years.

Average stock

The amount of stock held varies during the year: sometimes, such as during the Christmas period, stock will be high. The average stock held by a store is the quantity that is, on average, in the store at any one time. Of course, this varies from day to day. But, if you added the amounts of stock at the end of each day for, say, a year, and divided the total by the number of days, you would have the average stock. Imagine having to count stock after closing every day!

Normally, stocktaking is carried out once a year. At other times, stock is calculated from store records of sales and purchases.

The numbers of sales are deducted from the stock record, deliveries are added; the resulting figure should be the stock. To verify this, a physical stocktake is conducted.

Discrepancies will inevitably occur because of 'shrinkage'. Shrinkage is the term to denote the difference between actual stock and recorded stock. It arises because of undetected mistakes in deliveries, errors made in sales figures, and physical counting. Pilferage and shoplifting account for a very large percentage of shrinkage. We consider this in more detail in Chapter 14.

Average stock, as calculated from records, may be taken once a year, or more frequently. Where the levels of stocks are recorded monthly, a common method is to note the stock recorded at the end of each month, add 12 months' figures to the opening stock for

1st January and, because you have 13 quantities, divide the total by 13 to obtain average stock.

A cruder figure, when you only have opening and closing stock, is:

Average stock = (opening stock+plus closing stock)/2

In a store with annual sales of £3 million, the stock on 1st January was £560,000; on 31st December it was £640,000. The average stock was, therefore, £600,000 (560,000+640,000)/2.

While average stock is, to some extent, an estimate, you should appreciate its importance, because it has an impact on profits. Obviously, any money belonging to the store that is tied up in stock cannot be used for other purposes; if it could, it could be invested and interest earned on it. If it has been borrowed from the bank, then interest will have to be paid on it.

Thus, if the average stock held is £600,000, and interest is, say, 10 per cent a year, this stock costs the store £60,000 a year. That's just to pay interest on the value; there is also £600,000 tied up, and the cost of storage space.

Stock-turn

The time it takes for the amount of average stock to be sold is called stock-turn. Stock-turn is normally calculated for a year. With fresh fish, the stock-turn is about 300; that is, daily sales equal the value of average stock, or the average stock is sold every day. With jewellery, it is about 0.5, which means that about half the average stock is sold each year. For white goods—refrigerators, dishwashers, washing machines, deep freezers—stock-turn is around four.

Thus, the stock-turn for the store with annual sales of £3 million and average stock of £600,000 is five (3,000,000/600,000).

It follows that, by increasing stock-turn, we will have higher sales with lower average stock. This, in turn, means higher profit.

Percentages

The word 'percentage' means parts of a hundred. Thus, 25 parts of a hundred is 25 per cent. If you work on a profit of 30 per cent, it means that 30 parts of a hundred is profit.

SALES POLICY VERSUS PROFIT POLICY

This is convenient for comparing different things. If you make 25 per cent on wooden boxes, and 30 per cent on metal boxes, it's easy to see that metal boxes are more profitable. However, percentages can be confusing.

Supposing you sold two wooden boxes and one metal box, which is the more profitable? That is, two at 25 per cent profit or one at 30 per cent profit? Looked at one way, you could say that the metal box is still more profitable because you make 30 per cent on each one you sell. Tomorrow you might sell two metal boxes and no wooden boxes. It wouldn't affect the fact that metal boxes have a greater percentage profit.

Percentages conceal the true situation. If the wooden box is a handmade product and sells for £20, and the metal box is a small object selling at 60p, you can see immediately that 25 per cent of £20 is much better than 30 per cent of 60p. The wooden box, at 25 per cent, provides £5 profit; 30 per cent on the small metal box provides 18p profit.

We could conclude that wooden boxes are more profitable and, to make the same profit selling metal boxes as when selling one wooden box (£5), we would need to sell 28 (28 × 0.18 = £5.04).

Profit is more important than sales

It is not prudent to have just a sales policy; companies must have a profit policy. Simply making sales is not sufficient for a store to continue in business. Profit is what keeps companies in business. While you may not be able to contribute to the profit-making decisions, you can play your part in maintaining profit levels.

Supposing your personal sales figures are consistently high but you handle the products carelessly; they become shop-soiled. You set out displays without sufficient regard for the goods with the result that they have to be changed frequently. Your cost to the store would be much higher than someone who is careful with products. This could well account for the difference between a good profit and a poor profit.

Working all day for the store

Every time you do something during business hours that has nothing to do with the store and you keep customers waiting, frustrations will build up in customers who will then have a certain antipathy towards the store. You probably know of stores you like and those you try to avoid.

Every sale you fail to make because customers do not like to shop in your store is a loss of profit for the store. Every person you tend to 'turn off' your store is potential profit lost.

Look around your department or store and try to assess the amount of money required to start the operation, to hold all those stocks, pay all the salaries and expenses and the finance to keep the store in business.

Finance to keep a store operating

A lot of money is needed to keep the store running whether or not sales are made—rent, rates, insurance, lighting, heating, cleaning and so on. You can see how important it is to consider profit as well as sales. What would happen if sales kept on increasing but running costs kept rising faster? Sooner or later, drastic action would have to be taken, otherwise the store would 'go broke'. You might think that this is an exaggeration but this is precisely what happens to companies every day of the year. They are sales conscious rather than profit conscious.

Work for repeat sales

Make a definite effort to cultivate customers so that they will come back to do business with you, your department and your store. Few people buy all their needs from one store. Your task is to try to get them to buy the major items or the bulk of their needs from you.

If you are always pleasant and 'nothing is too much trouble', you will find that customers often return to buy from you. If you really know your products and can give sound advice to customers, they will want to be served by you. The advantage from the store's point of view is obvious. There is a better sales turnover and a higher stock-turn because regular customers buy more regularly and spend larger amounts each year than casual shoppers.

Customers will like you

This is reliable income and all because of the confidence you have created. The more your department and your store sells, the lower the cost of overheads (rent, rates, etc) per unit sale. There will also be real publicity value because satisfied customers tell their friends.

Part of your department may be self-selection. In such circumstances, it is often difficult to decide just when a customer wants help from you. If you wait for customers to ask, they may possibly think you are slow; if you approach them too quickly, they may think that you are pressurizing them.

Self-service

What is the objective of a self-selection department? It is to give customers the chance to browse at leisure and to cut down labour costs by letting customers make selections. You must be watchful to make sure that when a customer does want help or advice you can give it, but do not give the impression that you are waiting to pounce as soon as a product is looked at or picked up.

Remain relaxed and calm but look 'busy'. Walk near the customer, smile and make sure the customer knows that you are available. If you think it advisable, say, 'Good morning (afternoon)' and, if appropriate, ask 'Any luck?' 'All right, sir (madam)?', or 'We have several more in stock if you can't find what you are looking for.' Don't wait for an answer but stay close at hand and in sight. The customer will attract your attention if help or guidance is wanted. As soon as you see that a customer is interested in a selection, you can attempt to close the sale. Make sure that the product or item that the customer has selected is what is needed, but don't confuse the situation and offer alternative products.

Customer: (After looking at several products picks up a blue one and looks towards the salesman)
Salesman: All right, sir?
Customer: Yes. Thank you.
Salesman: Blue will be all right?
Customer: Yes. Yes, I think so.
Salesman: We have them in other colours. There's also green and brown here but I've some fawn and a darker green in stock.

Customer:	Oh! Dark green?
Salesman:	Yes, sir. Hold on. I'll just fetch one. (Disappears towards the rear of the store, and returns a few minutes later) Here you are sir, one in dark green and a couple in fawn.
Customer:	Hm!
Salesman:	They're attractive.
Customer:	Very. Do they do them in several colours?
Salesman:	Oh! Yes, sir. We stock about five or six. They're the most popular.
Customer:	Hm! (Obviously thinking) Do you have one in white?
Salesman:	We do normally, sir, but we're out of white at the moment.
Customer:	Ah! Y' know, I think I'll leave it for the moment and wait till you've got the white ones in. When do you have your next delivery?
Salesman:	Usually every month, sir.
Customer:	Well, thank you. Good morning.

And so the stock stays at the same level. While you must help customers, don't confuse them when they are reasonably satisfied with their choice of product. While your job is to help customers buy, don't put them off at the moment they have decided. It is not unknown for a customer to buy one, perhaps in blue, and later to buy a white one for someone else!

Comments by customers

Profit-minded sales people always listen to audible remarks made by one customer to another. This can be useful when two customers shop together. But never pass on comments made by one customer to another. You do not know why one person says something to another.

Supposing you heard a woman say to a child, 'No, Martin, they don't sell sweets in here.' Would you correct the woman if you knew that there was a large confectionery department on the next floor? Of course not. The woman might be saying that to deter the child.

Many times you will hear bits of conversation between people in your store that are incorrect. It is not part of your job to offer any enlightenment to those people.

SALES POLICY VERSUS PROFIT POLICY

If such a conversation is held in your presence, and the person who is giving the incorrect information knows that you know it is incorrect, you will build up confidence between you.

A social activity

Shopping is not simply a series of business transactions. It is a social activity indulged in by millions. All of us quite often 'go shopping' when we do not really wish to buy anything. We go to meet others, to have a cup of coffee or tea or to have a look at what is new.

You will find that you have a number of frequent customers, the 'regulars', walking through your store and, if you can manage to remember their names, you will be building confidence. Regulars will say to their friends, 'They know me there.' You won't be selling every minute of the day; a lot of your work will be contributing to the general running of your department: talking with customers who are only looking and not buying; giving advice to customers who want to visit other parts of the store; maintaining good relationships with customers. In other words, your aim will be profit-making rather than simply selling.

The telephone

You may have to answer the telephone. It may not be practical or possible for you to sell any of your products on the phone, but the way in which you answer callers will help to determine whether you can be called profit-conscious.

When you answer the telephone, make sure that the mouthpiece is completely in front of your mouth. Do not place it under your chin. Your lips should be very near to the mouthpiece so that the person at the other end will be able to hear you clearly. Speak with your normal voice and do not shout. In fact, if you put your mouth very close to the mouthpiece, you can speak in a much softer voice then usual, and people a few metres away will be unable to hear you talking with the caller.

Answering the phone

When you answer a telephone call, unless you have been instructed differently by your company, say 'Good morning (afternoon), such-and-such store or department, Miss Jones here' or 'Linda Jones here.' If you are a man, never use the word 'Mister' before your name; use your first name and surname, or your surname only. The only reason a woman uses 'Miss' or 'Mrs' is if she wishes the caller to know whether she is single or married. A number of women prefer to call themselves 'Ms'.

Be pleased to hear the caller

Always sound pleased to have a phone call. The fact that you have already answered the phone most of the morning is of no consequence to the caller who may well have been trying to phone you all morning! The caller may be in an irritable mood at getting the engaged tone all morning, but you must not reflect that mood.

A trick to use when answering the phone is to smile. Your voice will sound as though it is smiling.

When you pick up the receiver

One rule you should obey: always have a pad and something with which to write when you answer the phone.

Never pick up the receiver to answer the call without checking that you have a pencil, ball-point or other writing instrument and a pad of paper. Some organizations have special pads for recording all phone messages. Do not use bits of paper except in an emergency and then transfer the message onto a proper pad in writing that others can read!

Customers can be difficult

Customers can be as vague, awkward, talkative and time-consuming on the phone as they can be in the store. Never allow yourself to become irritated but try to give the caller all the help you can. Avoid being drawn into a discussion about a product that can only be sold by demonstration or a personal visit by the caller. Find out if it is possible for the caller to come into the store and, if so, to ask for you. Always note their name and telephone number.

If you have to say something to one of your colleagues while you are still on the phone, place your hand over the mouthpiece, covering it completely, but keep the earpiece to your ear.

If you have to make a business telephone call make sure you have pen, pad and all the facts in front of you so that you can be precise, brief and courteous. The company is paying for the call, the cost of which will eat into profits.

Being profit conscious

Profit-conscious sales people avoid waste, switch off unwanted lights, report damage to stock and fittings, however minor, as soon as discovered, and are careful with wrapping paper, bags and all those things that are not charged extra to the customer.

12
Increasing Sales

Selling more

We are mainly concerned here with increasing your personal sales but, as you will understand from the previous chapter, the profit-conscious sales person will also be concerned with increasing the sales of the whole store. Therefore, underlying one's own ideas must be the thought that one's department is part of the total store and, where possible, customers should be encouraged to visit other departments. You must not give the impression that your department is the only one that counts.

You can increase your sales in a number of ways; some are directly within your control, others are not, although you can contribute to their success.

How to increase your sales

The easiest and quickest way to increase your sales is to sell something extra to a customer already making a purchase. A customer buys a coat and you also sell a scarf. A man buys a tape recorder. He will also need tapes, and why not a cleaning tape? He will certainly need a plug and, if one is not fitted to the apparatus, as it is on the continent, he may need to buy one.

Salesman: Right, sir. You have the recorder and half-a-dozen tapes. You'll need a plug; do you have one?
Customer: Yes, thank you.
Salesman: With a three-amp fuse?
Customer: Ah! I don't know.

Salesman:	Well, don't use a five-amp and certainly not a thirteen-amp, that's much too big and won't protect your machine adequately.
Customer:	I think I'd better take a new one.
Salesman:	Yes, sir. There we are. Now, after you've been playing it for about 20 hours, it's advisable to clean the head and demagnetize it. If you don't, the reproduction will deteriorate. Clean the head with a little methylated spirit on cotton wool on a match stick. Open it like this. (Demonstrates) Press the record button so that you can see the heads here (Points) and gently clean them. Just a few seconds.
Customer:	Well, thank you. And that will demagnetize it.
Salesman:	No, sir. That will clean it. It will remove the build-up of dust and small particles. You only need to demagnetize it about every 40 hours or so.
Customer:	How do I do that?
Salesman:	With this cleaning tape, sir. (Places one on the counter) It will also keep the head clean.
Customer:	How much is it?
Salesman:	£2.50, sir.
Customer:	Oh! I may as well take one now. Thank you.

Essential or natural pairing

A woman buys a new saucepan; she might need a cooking thermometer, whisk, spatula, or some item she may have mentioned in your conversation with her. A man buys an umbrella and you might consider trying to sell him a pair of waterproofed overtrousers. But not everything should be paired together in this way. It is only when the item is a natural accessory: a matching tie with the shirt; extra shoe laces and polish with shoes; a service agreement to extend the guarantee period with a video recorder; twist and masonry bits with an electric drill; spares with almost any equipment.

To attempt to sell a hat to a customer who has bought a coat is not good pairing. Good pairing is selling a plastic cover for use when the coat is hanging in the wardrobe.

130 RETAIL SELLING

Complementary not competitive accessories

If a man buys an umbrella, to attempt to sell him a pair of waterproof over-trousers as well is not the way to increase sales.

Salesman: That is the best, sir. It's an English frame and an attractive whangee handle.
Customer: Fine. How much is that one?
Salesman: £35. Including tax.
Customer: Okay.
Salesman: Would you like it in a container, sir, or will you take it as it is?
Customer: I'll take it as it is, thank you.
Salesman: Very well, sir. (Places invoice pad in front of him and prepares to write out the bill) While you are here, you might like to see these. (Introduces a pair of water-proofed over-trousers on the counter) They're very light and clip onto the trouser pockets. Stops the rain from getting at the bottom of the trousers.
Customer: How interesting. I thought they didn't make these anymore.
Salesman: I haven't seen them for years, but they are coming back. They're so handy in town.
Customer: Only in this colour?
Salesman: No. There's that fawn, this olive green, and er—black. (Places two other packs on the counter) The three colours.
Customer: (Inspecting the unwrapped pair closely) How much are they?
Salesman: £5.50, sir.
Customer: You know, that's just what I want. I drive all the time and don't really need an umbrella; it's just for getting out of the car in the rain and walking to an office. I'll tell you what, I'll leave the umbrella for now, and take a pair of these. They're much more suitable and will save me quite a bit.
Salesman: (A little disappointed but not showing it) Certainly, sir. No problem. I'm glad we thought of them.

When you have sold something to a customer, and that customer is ready to pay, do not confuse the issue and introduce a product that competes with the one the customer is buying. Only introduce those products that are natural, or essential, accessories or pairings.

However, it is sometimes good policy to sell a less costly product if it is appropriate and if, in your opinion, it will satisfy the customer as well as, or more than, the more expensive product. One thing is for sure—that customer will want to buy from you again because you have helped the customer to buy rather than simply selling something. You have sold the customer what was really needed.

Here are some of the things to say to customers after a purchase has been made:

- Is that everything?
- Is that all?
- Is there anything else?
- Is there something else I can show you?
- Nothing else? (Probably the most negative)

These comments are a sort of signing-off language made by retail sales people when a sale has been made. The sale was started, progressed and has now been completed. There is a feeling of accomplishment, and the transaction has been ended. Thus, 'Will that be all?' tends to come naturally.

When to stop?

We cannot continue trying to sell a customer article after article; we have to stop somewhere. The question is, when do we stop? If we sell a man a coat, and a hat, do we then offer a scarf; a shirt; a tie; cuff links? There has to be an end to it, otherwise the customer runs out of money! More realistically, if we always try to sell something else, we get the reputation for high pressure selling. In general, this will have a negative effect and keep customers away.

The professional sales person will sell the customer what that customer really needs. Sometimes, customers do not know what they really need; only what they think they want. Your aim must be to sell them products that will satisfy those needs. These you must ascertain from the conversation during your sales presentation.

Unless the customer tells you that they need a variety of goods, you should only sell additional articles which are natural complements—accessories, spares, cleaners, etc.

> Customer: Good afternoon. I should like to see some shirts, please. Cotton, 15½.
> Salesman: Certainly, sir. Any particular colour?
> Customer: Not sure, really. Not blue, though.
> Salesman: Let me show you one or two to give you an idea of style and design. (He notes that the customer is a youngish man with modern cut clothes) Here are three different styles. This one is traditional, it will never really look out of place. This one has a slightly more modern cut, a long pointed collar but not too long to date it; this one is a fairly new trend; we haven't had them in very long. They are designed to be worn with or without a tie and the collar may be buttoned down, as you can see.

The salesman is really asking the customer 'what kind of shirt are you looking for?' because he is trying to find out what the customer needs.

> Customer: I don't think this one. (Points to the traditional shirt) I have plenty of these. But I like both of these. How much are they?
> Salesman: (Judging that price is not an obstacle, treats the price almost as incidental) This one, £18 and this £22. (Still trying to find out what the customer needs) Do you want it for everyday wear or a particular occasion?

Note two things about the salesman's question. Firstly, he uses the word 'particular' rather than 'special' occasion because he judges that this customer does not keep clothes for special occasions, and just wears what is suitable in his wardrobe. Some people have suits or dresses regarded as their 'best suit' or 'best dress' for wear on special occasions. Others do not have specially categorized clothes.

People who wear formal clothes during the week tend to wear casual clothes at the weekend. Those who have to wear protective clothing, or work clothes during the week, tend to wear slightly more 'formal' clothes at weekends, and would regard some suits and dresses as 'best' clothes.

Secondly, the salesman used the word 'occasions' in the plural rather than the singular, which would imply that he was buying a shirt for one particular occasion. The implication is that the customer is used to going to particular occasions.

Customer: Not really. I want a new shirt that I can wear to a 'do'. Not formal. Want to look—er—y' know...
Salesman: 'With it', without being flashy. (Finishing the customer's sentence)
Customer: That's right.
Salesman: (Still searching for information) What do you prefer now when you go to, say, a weekend get-together?
Customer: Well, I don't have anything really. Except the sort of shirts I wear everyday.
Salesman: (Decides the customer really needs two shirts and a matching tie for one) Let's consider this one. (Taking another shirt from the drawer) It's quite modern and yet has a certain something. Might I suggest a slightly darker shade though? (Gets another shirt from the drawer) It looks better when worn without a tie.
Customer: Hmm! Very attractive. I like that.

The salesman continues to sell the customer *what the customer really needs*, and not just a shirt. Having established what is needed, he will now sell a tie to go with the shirt and possibly another, slightly more formal shirt, that could be carried as a spare. He is selling a package rather than selling one item and then another.

If you can do this on only a proportion of your sales, you will increase your sales turnover considerably. Avoid making suggestions such as:

Customer: Thank you. I'll take this one, the grey.
Salesman: Thank you, sir. What about a nice matching tie?

The customer will say 'no' automatically. Let's try it a different way:

134   RETAIL SELLING

Customer: Thank you. I'll take this one, the grey.
Salesman: Thank you, sir. (Selecting a tie from a nearby rack) Don't you think that this matches it very well, sir?

Customer thinks that the salesman is now trying to get him to buy something else. It's a sales ploy! If he says 'yes', he is going to be under pressure to buy it. But he can't say 'no', because it does match! A different approach:

Customer: Thank you I'll take this one, the grey.
Salesman: Thank you, sir. Wouldn't you say a new shirt deserves a new tie, sir?
Customer: Probably, but no, thank you. (These chaps are always trying to sell. Have to be careful.)

Avoid making suggestions like these. It is better to find out what the customer really needs. If he gets home and finds that with his new shirt, the only tie that would match is soiled, old and out-of-date, he will not have achieved what he has been trying to achieve. Therefore, help the customer to buy. Here is the above sales situation handled slightly differently:

Customer: Thank you. I'll take this one, the grey.
Salesman: Thank you, sir. I assume we have a tie to go with it? It doesn't want to be too 'busy'.

The customer has to think about this. The use of the 'we' is helping the customer to buy. The salesman is not trying to sell him a tie, he is asking whether the customer will be able to achieve his objective. He is also making the customer decide whether the tie he might have been thinking of using was 'busy'. The salesman *does not* even show him a tie! Here is another approach used by an experienced salesman at a men's shop in Bournemouth:

Customer: Thank you. I'll take this one, the grey.
Salesman: Thank you, sir. By the way, next time you're in or, if someone wants to give you a present, I have just the tie that will go with that shirt. (Slight pause) Now, may I put your name on the bill, sir?

Here is a subtle way of selling the tie; the salesman doesn't even show it. His attitude assumes that the customer is not going to buy the tie then, but he is making sure that the customer knows he

INCREASING SALES

has a record of the sale so that he can produce the tie later when needed! What did this customer say?

Customer: Can I have a look at it now?
Salesman: (Does not produce tie immediately but leaves the customer for several seconds. Returns with tie. Places folded tie, to give the impression of being knotted, on the front of the shirt. *He says nothing!* But he has carefully placed the price ticket so that it will just show at the end of the tie.)
Customer: I think I'll take it now.
Salesman: As you wish, sir. Thank you.

All of which seems to agree with the principle that when you have made your point, shut up. Say nothing. Because the first one who speaks after that loses!

You cannot sell something to someone that they do not want. Therefore you have to develop your skill of salesmanship by helping customers to buy. In this way you will increase your personal sales.

13
The Store's Image and Prices

Creating the image

To some extent, every retail outlet specializes in the range of goods it offers, the category of people to whom it aims to sell, the price levels of its products, and by a combination of publicity appeals. In this way, an 'image' is created in the mind of the general public. Your store projects its own unique or particular image to the public. Doubtless, before you joined the company, you had a certain feeling for the store, an overall impression of it and of the part of it where you would work.

This is the image created by the type and quality of products, the way they are displayed and presented for sale, the layout and procedures in the whole establishment, and even the way the employees speak to you.

Most multiples and chains maintain this image throughout all their branches by means of their 'livery'. The livery is the combined effect of the shop-front, the colour scheme, the type of lettering for the name, the delivery vans, uniforms or work clothes where supplied, letter-headings, and display notices. The windows and interior displays are identical in general layout, and it is difficult to tell one branch from another. You can visit a W H Smith, Boots the Chemist, Tesco's, Sainsbury's or Halfords in one town and not detect a great deal of difference from their branches in another part of the country.

To the company the value of creating this image is that customers will be at ease, familiar with the interior store layout, the products, buying procedures and staff attitudes, irrespective of which branch they visit. The only general difference is in the amount and range of stock carried. Obviously, a large branch can carry a wider selection of types, models and sizes of the same products than a small branch. But the standard, the image, is the same.

Whether you work in one small, independent shop, a group with three or four branches, a large department store, or a multiple chain, you are part of the image. The way you look, the manner in which you deal with customers, how you help them to satisfy their needs when buying your company's products, how you write out the invoice, accept their charge or credit card or hand back change after a transaction all contribute to the company's image.

It takes a long time to build an image. It can be dented, and even destroyed, very quickly.

The intangible image

An image is largely intangible. It is a certain combination of things that together give a similar impression to most people. Sometimes, this image is the same for all people; sometimes they are sharply divided in their opinion of an image of something or someone. You only have to consider the image of politicians; the same politican will project an image to his or her supporters diametrically opposed to that held by the opposition.

You can have an opinion about the image of something without ever having experienced it. For example, you probably have an image of the moon or, nearer home, the western desert of Australia, or Siberia in the Soviet Union, but it is unlikely that you have ever been to any of them.

Harrods, of Knightsbridge, London, has an image; the Beatles had an image; the 1914-18 war had an image; a Rolls Royce has an image; Marks and Spencer has an image. These images have all been built up by many contributions, not the least of which are the attitudes of people intimately involved with them.

If you own or work in the smallest of 'corner' shops, it has an image in the minds of the local people.

Image is difficult to change

When I was with Moss Bros of Covent Garden, the image of the store and its branches was, and possibly still is today, of a hire company. They hire out evening wear, morning wear, and other things for special occasions. It used to be said that you could always tell a Moss Bros hired evening suit or morning wear, because it was the best cut, best tailored suit in the gathering. It was even said that it would not be possible to hold a coronation without Moss Bros because they hired out all the robes and coronets. All part of the Moss Bros image.

My task, when I joined them, was to try to change their image from a hire company to a company that made and sold the finest tailored clothes. It was an uphill struggle. It proved almost impossible to change the image of the store. We had dozens of advertisements announcing suits for sale, riding wear for sale, ski wear for sale, evening wear for sale, morning wear for sale, shoes, briefcases, gloves, socks, shirts, ties, women's dresses, everything for sale. But it took just one advertisement for hire wear to negate all the other advertising.

We had a standard cartoon advertisement for theatre programmes. It pictured the whole audience in evening dress except one man in the front row in an ordinary suit. The words under the cartoon: 'Surely he's heard of Moss Bros!' The message was that it was easy to hire from us.

I decided to use the theme but change the emphasis so that it would apply to clothes for sale. I placed an advertisement on the back page of the *Daily Telegraph* for the Moss Bros riding macintosh, a superb waterproof coat. It was a cartoon of several people sitting comfortably dry on their horses during a heavy rain storm, but with one very despondent looking rider, rain leaking in everywhere. The caption was: 'Surely he's heard of the Moss Bros raincoat!'

A number of people phoned to tell me about the amusing cartoon that had been published about us. It wasn't an editorial cartoon, it was an advertisement. What I had not been able to project was that we sold raincoats; the image was still that we hired them.

On another occasion, there was a genuine editorial cartoon in *Punch* with a man at the cloakroom of a large hotel asking for his top hat. He was saying to the attendant who was standing before countless racks of top hats, 'It's the one with a Moss Bros label in it!' The implication was that every one of the top hats had a similar label.

We had agreed to the use of our name with the Boulting Brothers who were producing a film about a wedding. After a series of mishaps, the unfortunate bridegroom, played by Ian Carmichael, appeared before the local magistrates on the morning of his wedding. Dressed in his morning suit, he faced the magistrate who

THE STORE'S IMAGE AND PRICES

was handed a card by the clerk of the court. The magistrate read the card aloud and slowly, 'Return to Moss Bros by Thursday morning'. He continued, 'Another displaced Yugoslav, I suppose!'

There were many other incidents as well which impressed on me the difficulty of changing an image.

Selling is a creative activity

Selling is a creative activity and you should not be content simply to show goods, wrap them and take the money. An automatic slot machine could do that! You can help to build a good image for your department and for your store by the creativity with which you approach your task.

Perhaps the most sensitive area where the image of the store will manifest itself will be in the quality and price range of your products. You should always be able to deal with problems raised about price.

Problem of price

It is generally agreed that price is one of the most difficult features to cope with. There are really two aspects of this matter of price: the value represented by the price being asked, and the total outlay involved. It is sometimes held that value, in terms of the quality for the price asked, is more important than the price itself.

It may be so. But you try telling this to a customer who has only £5 to spare to buy something. She will not be the slightest bit interested in your argument that a particular article at £10 is superb value. So don't waste your time in trying to convince customers that value is the important thing when they have a limited amount of money to spend.

Fortunately, the majority of customers are not so restricted and, with the usual services offered by most shops—budgeted purchasing, extended credit and hire purchase—price is not so critical. In fact, price comes pretty low on the list of motives that influence customers. The question that arises in customers' minds is, 'Is it worth the money?'

When do you mention price?

The question often asked is, when should the price be mentioned in the sales presentation? There is no single answer. Every customer wants to know the price 'bracket' or 'area' of the product. It's no good waiting until the end of the sales presentation and then telling the customer that the price is something way beyond what he or she is willing to spend.

Let the customer know early in your sales presentation what price area you are in. It is a waste of time being skilful in your presentation and then finding that you could have been just as skilful with a product in a price bracket desired by the customer.

The price bracket

A good example of the use of price is with cameras. They range from a few pounds to a thousand or more. If a man expresses an interest in buying a camera from you, what questions do you want answered? Those that will find out what he really needs, such as speed and focal length of lens, whether he needs an automatic shutter, automatic focusing, computer-controlled mechanism, built-in flash, and so on. He wants to obtain the best value he can for the amount of money he has in mind. He may know a lot about cameras and their prices, and have seen the advertisements, or he may know little.

The way you handle this situation will help shape your shop's image. There would be little sense in showing him the wide versatility of a very expensive camera in which he shows considerable interest—who wouldn't!—and he then says, 'Most interesting. Now, what I'm looking for is something around £30.'

There is no need to announce the price of everything you show, but the customer must have a good idea of their range of prices. Some people advise that you should never ask a customer how much he or she wishes to spend. But if your range of models of a product is from, say, £5 to £500, it makes good sense to say to the customer, 'Our range is from a few pounds to many hundreds. What area are you thinking of?'

The question, 'About how much do you want to spend?' is almost in the same category as, 'Can I help you?' Yet, you must know in which price bracket the customer is prepared to buy.

THE STORE'S IMAGE AND PRICES 141

If you place two products in front of the customer and say that one costs £5 and the other £20, you will most likely be asked for something 'in between'. So why not start with something in between? Show the average priced product and say that you can show something more, or less, costly. This helps to create a good image; you are helping the customer.

Price is part of the sale

Price is part of every sale. It is not something that raises its head every now and again: it is always present. Never be afraid of stating the price when asked. You may think that the product is high priced, even expensive, but to stay in business, your shop has to be as keen in its particular market as its competitors.

Customers who patronize your shop will normally have a general idea of the price range of your goods because of the image that has been built up over the years. It is also common to display all goods with prices clearly marked. Some shops use price lining—that is, goods displayed in price ranges.

If a customer says, 'It seems a lot of money' or 'It's rather expensive', you could say, 'Madam (sir), surely it's a question of value.' What the customer is actually saying is that it is a lot of money compared with the level he or she had in mind before seeing the product.

This is a sensitive area and, if you handle the situation well, it will help in creating a good image for you and your store. Avoid saying, 'You get what you pay for.' Not only is it trite, it does not help the customer to buy. Use questions to find out if the customer has purchased a similar product recently; what price they had in mind and what was their reference for that price. If appropriate, find out the intended purpose of the product. Explore the reasons why the customer thinks that the price is high.

In order to attract customers to a store, sometimes the lowest priced products are advertised. This can give customers the idea that all similar products are around the same price. Very few stores advertise their most expensive products, and the general tendency is to advertise the lower quality products in order to stimulate interest. You may visit the store and have a look at the low priced products that have been advertised, but then prefer to purchase a better, higher priced, product.

Barrier technique applied to price

If a customer says that the price is rather high, you can use the barrier erecting technique to deal with this and pay the customer a compliment at the same time.

>Saleswoman: The kind of quality you are demanding, sir (madam) can only be obtained by paying considerably more.
>
>Salesman: The standard you want, sir (madam) is going to cost you in the region of — (naming a much higher figure).

The customer cannot then jump back over the barrier without admitting that a lower quality is wanted and, at the same time, has to imply that your price is reasonable. The following conversation is a condensed version of what took place in a department store in Canterbury, Kent.

>Customer: We want a carpet for our sitting room.
>
>Salesman: As you can see we have a variety of types, madam. What size would you need?
>
>Customer: I think it's twelve by nine.
>
>Salesman: What do you have at the moment, madam?
>
>Customer: Ah! It's a very old carpet. Going threadbare in places.
>
>Salesman: Do you know what make or type it is?
>
>Customer: Not really, except that it's very old.
>
>Salesman: (Walking toward the display) What is the main colour we have to look for?
>
>Customer: Well, the furniture is covered in old gold Dralon.
>
>Salesman: Is it a new house or an old one?
>
>Customer: Quite old. Like the furniture! Actually it's a period house so we want a carpet similar to the one we have now. Perhaps a 'sad' blue colour might be suitable.
>
>Salesman: Let me turn back a few of these to show the kind of designs you might find interesting.
>
>Customer: What size is that one?
>
>Salesman: Twelve by nine.
>
>Customer: What price is it?
>
>Salesman: £699.

Customer:	(Astonished) That's £700!
Salesman:	By the time you have the underlay — I take it you would need a new one — it would be about £900.
Customer:	Good gracious.
Salesman:	You see, madam, the kind of quality you are looking for cannot be obtained cheaply. I daresay you've had your present carpet for a good many years.
Customer:	Yes. Ever since we were married. But it didn't cost anywhere near £900. (Pauses reflectively) I expected it would be about a couple of hundred pounds.
Salesman:	Judging from what you say and from the use you have had from it I would say it was of first class quality. To get the same quality today you would have to pay about a thousand. However, if you would like to see something less expensive, I can show you, but I don't think you're going to be satisfied. If you pay a couple of hundred pounds you're not going to get what you want.
Customer:	Hmm!
Salesman:	£900 is a lot of money by anyone's standards. On the other hand, we do have an extended credit scheme that makes it easier to cope with. However, before we go into that, what do you think of this design and colour?
Customer:	I think it's perfect. It would go very well with the furniture.
Salesman:	Old furniture, you said, madam?
Customer:	Yes. Well, antique really.
Salesman:	(Realizes that the customer cannot be allowed to buy a cheap carpet from him because it would not be satisfactory and would only reflect on the store generally) There's no way you're going to get satisfaction from a £200 carpet, madam. It wouldn't look well against your furniture. It would be better to stay with your present one. However, before you decide to have this one. I would suggest we arrange to deliver it, put it down and you can see how it fits in. By the way, where do you live?

Customer: (Gives address)
Salesman: If you're going to invest £700 in a carpet we would prefer that you have it down first to see if you are entirely satisfied. This particular carpet will give you at least 30 years' service. In fact, it is the same quality that is laid in some hotel public rooms. It is one hundred per cent pure wool. Now I suggest we let you have a look at it at home. We deliver in your area (consulting his card) Fridays. Would next Friday be convenient?

The barrier is built

Do you see how this customer cannot go back over the barrier that the salesman has erected concerning quality and the standard she is used to having? When your customer says that a product seems to be expensive it will be mostly because of lack of knowledge of the market. The woman buying the carpet only really knew the value of carpets she might have bought years ago and has probably seen adverts in local papers for carpets of a much inferior quality.

The price image

Supposing your store advertised products in the highest price bracket—the most expensive cameras, the most costly video recorders, the most expensive fur coats, the most expensive dresses, the most expensive menswear and so on. The image would be one of exclusivity and not many of the general mass of people would be drawn to the store because they would think it too expensive.

Conversely, if your store advertised the lowest priced articles, it would project an entirely different image.

Most stores try to keep a balance between low and high priced products so that customers are able to buy the ones they have seen advertised or can select more, or less, expensive products.

THE STORE'S IMAGE AND PRICES

How to mention price

Opinions differ as to how you should mention price: whether on its own or coupled with a statement of a customer benefit.

If we consider what generally takes place in a customer's mind when the price is mentioned, this may help. You state the price; the customer is either pleased, neutral, or disappointed.

Suppose you are showing a product to a man and the subject of price is raised; you tell him how much it is. If he is pleased, then price is not a barrier to buying; if he is not worried one way or the other, that is, neutral, then price is still not a barrier to buying.

If he is disappointed, however, no matter what you have linked with the price, he will be disappointed because, at the point when he learns the price, his preconception of price is stronger than the customer benefit.

His preconception of the price influences his judgement, and his disappointment is, initially, an obstacle preventing the appreciation of any customer benefit.

From here, the customer begins a tussle with himself. The very fact that he is disappointed at the 'high' price means that at that point he is interested mainly in price level.

To couple any customer benefit with a statement of price has little value and, at worst, could be misconstrued as an attempt to justify the price. Therefore, you are advised to state the price and say nothing else.

Salesman: Here is the product you were asking to see, sir.
Customer: Ah! Thank you. How much is it?
Salesman: £28, and that includes a year's free service.

If this customer thought the product was around £10 his disappointment will prevent him from appreciating the value of a year's free service. The benefit of the free service has now been stated in a negative way; it has been given too early.

It is better to state the price and keep the benefit of the free service for positive use later in the presentation. Let the customer hear the price and work on his disappointment in his own way. Use the 'year's free service' and other customer benefits positively to help him win his inner tussle and enable him to purchase at the price he thought, at one stage, was too high.

Defending the price

Never defend the price! When the customer tells you that the price is high, there is a natural tendency to want to defend it; don't! It is not something to be ashamed of; it is not something you have to defend. To attempt to defend the price is to apologize for it being too high. You are trying to defend the image of your store!

In fact, the customer should not expect to obtain products at anything less than their reasonable price.

Of course, you can't say this. You can't say, 'I'm sorry, but it is expensive.' Who are you sorry for? For yourself? For the customer? Or for the people who made it? A high price does not mean over-priced and you do not need to defend it.

The prices you charge in your store reflect your general image. They are the result of good, competitive buying, plus all the additional services customers expect from a modern retail establishment. The price of a product should cause you no more trouble than its colour, size or the materials of which it is made.

14
Service and Shrinkage

The concept of service

No one buys a product for itself alone but for the satisfaction, or service, it provides. A washing machine is of little value until it is washing clothes. That is the reason it is purchased: to wash clothes. If it does so automatically, so much the better. Similarly a dish washer is providing no service until it is being used to wash dishes.

Every product we purchase provides a service or satisfies us in some way. It performs some function, or gives us the pleasure of ownership, such as with glass paperweights, postage stamps, cigarette cards, rare coins, gold sovereigns, old china plates, and other things we collect.

This is one meaning of service; it is similar to satisfaction. Products that don't actually do anything provide satisfaction of ownership. Even a picture that hangs on the wall provides its owner with the satisfaction of looking at it and enjoying it. The picture doesn't do anything, it just hangs there. But the satisfaction, and probably pleasure, is in being able to see and admire it.

Products that perform functions—wash clothes, dig the garden, play music, relay radio programmes, make holes in wood, stone or steel, type documents, calculate electronically, process writing onto a video screen, transmit images over telephone links and such things—provide services. We buy them because of the service and not because of themselves alone.

Another meaning of service is what we provide customers. This can be given before, during, or after, their purchase.

Before-sales service

There are a great many services provided for customers before

148 RETAIL SELLING

they have bought anything. Heating, lighting, toilets, etc, are all part of the general service available to those who visit the store, whether or not they buy.

There are also a number of specific services provided, normally without cost, before the customer has decided to buy.

The salesman who offered to deliver the carpet to the customer so that she could see what it looked like before she decided to buy it, is providing a before-sales service. Any customer who is thinking of buying a carpet or carpeting can expect the store to send someone to measure the room, leave a selection of carpet samples, and give a quotation for supplying and laying whatever is selected.

Literature is provided; queries are answered over the phone; advice is given freely by qualified staff; demonstrations are made in the store and at a potential buyer's premises or home. Bathrooms and kitchens are designed; garden layouts are prepared with recommended plants, shrubs and flowers, suggestions are offered for home extensions; equipment is loaned on trial. All these and many others are part of before-sales service.

During-sales service

When you are in the process of selling something to a customer, you are providing a service. You are telling the customer about the product, how and where it is made, what it is made of, how it will perform or wear; you show the product, possibly demonstrate how it fits together or works and answer questions.

Often, you will use sample or demonstration products not provided by the manufacturer, but taken from stock. These are used to show to customers during the process of selling.

If you have undergone any form of retail sales training for your job, your skills and ability are being developed for use during the sale. The service you can provide customers when you are making your sales presentation will help to persuade them to buy from you.

Self-service and full-service

Retail outlets operate one of two main sales procedures: self-selection or full-service. Self-selection may also be self-service

SERVICE AND SHRINKAGE   149

where customers are free to walk around the store and to inspect and handle the products. When they have chosen the goods, they take them to a special counter and pay for them. They only receive assistance from sales people when they ask for it.

In some stores, customers receive a degree of personal service. Sales people handle, show or demonstrate the product and, when the sale is made, complete the sales invoice. The sales person writes out the sales slip and the customer pays for the goods at a central point. In other outlets, a full, personal service is provided: the sale is completed entirely by the sales person who handles cash, or the credit arrangements, receipts the bill, gives the customer any change, and generally completes the sales transaction.

Self-selection products are well protected from frequent handling and are normally products that can be easily inspected, are not complicated and do not need to be demonstrated.

Full-service selling is necessary with complex products and those which would quickly deteriorate if handled too often. Originally, foodstuffs were sold by a full-service operation: each shopkeeper would handle the product: they would count or weigh, pack and seal, and complete each separate transaction. The time and labour involved in weighing or counting individual amounts of tea, sugar, butter, rice, cheese, flour etc made the weekly shopping expedition very time consuming. Turnover and profits were restricted by the number of individual sales.

With increasing labour costs, higher taxes, and the subsequent need to generate greater profits from capital invested in stores, the development of improved packing and packaging materials facilitated the change to self-service operations. This greatly increased sales and profit of stores. Individual transactions do not require the attention of sales staff, and customers can be left to themselves to view and select merchandise; staff are needed to give occasional help, and cashiers to wrap products and take money from customers. A new category of staff emerged: those whose job it is to keep the shelves filled and tidy.

You may work in either type of store; service is important in both. In the open-plan store, where customers wander around and inspect the goods, you may be asked to give advice and even be drawn into discussions with customers. This is all part of the service aspect of retail selling.

In the full-service store in which you have to serve customers, you can understand why it is important to show customers a range of products that you can count almost on one hand. It may even be a rule in your department not to have more than a certain number of items on show to a customer at any one time. While this is easy to understand, it is often difficult when you have many customers to serve.

Shrinkage

A hidden form of service you can perform to customer and store alike is to play your part in the reduction of 'shrinkage' of goods. Goods that are constantly shown, or demonstrated, to customers gradually become shop-soiled. They cannot be sold as new products and have to be sold at a fraction of their normal cost. Some products are actually used up when being shown to customers so that the store has less of them to sell.

With products which are cut to lengths or sizes demanded by the customer, such as fabric, floor-coverings, wood, electric cable etc, there are often remainders that cannot be sold at the full price and have to be sold as 'ends'. These are all part of the accepted shrinkage factor in retailing. The shopkeeper might purchase a hundred of a certain product, but normal shrinkage might permit only 98, 97, or fewer to be fit for sale. You can contribute to the reduction of this form of shrinkage by the careful way in which you handle products.

Other forms of shrinkage are more serious. They include:

- Short deliveries to the store
- Mistakes in recording of deliveries
- Products damaged and not noticed in good time
- Pilferage by staff
- Theft by customers.

Every store in every country suffers from shrinkage. Here is one manager telling a new trainee about the facts of life in their store.

Manager: Retailing has changed dramatically in this trade. The shopkeeper used to know all his customers; the assortment of goods was much smaller, and the family usually lent a hand when times were busy.
Trainee: Today it's quite different.

SERVICE AND SHRINKAGE

Manager: Yes. Today, retailing is an organized team job with the manager, department heads for the different product groups, supervisors, check-out staff, shelf-fillers, and others. We have to work as a team; make sure we buy the right type of products in good time to achieve a large enough profit to keep the store in business.

Trainee: What is gross profit?

Manager: Gross profit is the difference between what we pay for a product and what we sell it for. But from gross profit, we have to deduct all the expenses; what's left is net profit. Oh! And we act as tax collectors; we have to deduct value added tax from the price before anything else.

Trainee: How much profit do we make on average?

Manager: Well, let's work on a price of, say, 100. Tax accounts for 15 per cent; the cost of the product, on average, for, say, 50 per cent. Wages, admin, sales and social security costs account for 18 per cent; seven per cent for rent, interest and depreciation, five per cent for publicity leaving us with three per cent net profit.

Trainee: But I make that only 98 per cent!

Manager: Exactly! Two per cent just vanishes into thin air. It's shrinkage.

Trainee: Do you mean to say that the amount of wastage, or shrinkage, is nearly as big as the net profit?

Manager: Yes. Competition is so tough these days that net profit is only about three per cent, and we lose two per cent in shrinkage: mainly shoplifting.

    It means that for every stolen item, we need to sell 50 in order to compensate for the loss: we only make profit on the additional ones we manage to sell.

Trainee: Then how can we increase our net profit?

Manager: Well, we can boost sales but, as you know, this is not easy. If we spend extra on advertising, store promotions and other publicity, we cannot guarantee that sales will increase sufficiently. For example, if we spend, say, £1,000 on a special promotion, at three per cent net profit, we need to generate approximately an additional £33,000 in turnover just to pay for the promotion.

Trainee: Modern retailing is not that simple, then.

Manager: No. Retailers can't avoid wastage when they are left with parts of products, or have to trim meat, remove jaded fruit and vegetables, sell off soiled stock; and it's only human to break something now and again. But all this is visible shrinkage. It can't be avoided; yet it accounts for only about a quarter of the total shrinkage. The big problem is invisible shrinkage. It amounts to about 1½ per cent of turnover. Just think: we have a total sales turnover of about £20 million and we have an invisible shrinkage of £300,000 a year!

Trainee: But you said it's invisible. How do you know it?

Manager: It's quite easy to calculate the sales value we had during a certain period and subtract the amount of money that was actually received. The difference is shrinkage. Of course, we have to allow for the products in stock. That's one of the reasons for stocktaking.

Trainee: Shoplifting is responsible for the invisible shrinkage?

Manager: No, it's not that simple. Invisible shrinkage is not only because of theft by customers; we are also responsible. When we don't observe and correct wrong deliveries and invoices; when we are slipshod with price-marking and careless making price changes; when we make wrong recordings on cash tills. All these contribute to shrinkage. Occasionally, even a member of staff can fall into temptation and commit, shall we say, irregularities? It can happen through cooperating with friends or suppliers, and with staff purchases.

All shrinkage affects the staff, the store and, in the long run, the customers. If shrinkage is too high, a store runs at a loss instead of a profit and this can end in bankruptcy. It was estimated by excessive shrinkage.

While a number of technical measures can be taken—mirrors, closed circuit television, plainclothes store detectives, alarms etc—the main way to fight the shoplifters is by the general service provided by the staff. Effective working and checking routines give staff and customers confidence in the store.

Shoplifting

You cannot tell in advance from a customer's appearance that he or she is about to leave the store with goods not paid for. Shoplifters do not belong to any special category of people. They could be anyone.

However, the worst offenders are the professional shoplifters who work in pairs and teams. They make a 'living' out of stealing from retail outlets and make careful preparations, concentrating usually on the more expensive, easy-to-carry products. You are unlikely to spot the professionals; but the security people in your store will have been trained to deal with such professional shoplifters.

There is one type of shoplifter who takes something, perhaps on the spur of the moment, even something they do not need. Although the goods may not be expensive, the total amount of such thefts can add up to serious losses.

The most common form of shoplifting is to put an article into the pocket or bag. A slightly more sophisticated technique is to use a folded newspaper or umbrella, or simply to place a small article inside a larger one. Some thieves exchange price labels, presenting the expensive product with the low price ticket to the sales person.

All stores have shoplifters and, sooner or later, some are detected. Then it is an unpleasant situation for all concerned, especially if the shoplifter is not a professional but has taken something on the spur of the moment.

Prevention is better than cure; this is one of the reasons for a particular store's layout. Attractive, expensive goods are displayed in a way that they can be easily observed. Mirrors and closed circuit television cover the more inaccessible or hidden areas. Uniformed security people walking round the store are most useful for prevention because they are constantly on view. Plainclothes detectives are employed to catch the habitual or professional shoplifters.

Alert staff can provide a valuable service to combat shoplifting. You should circulate in your area as much as possible; look and smile at customers rather than stand talking with colleagues.

Action to take with a shoplifter

Your store manager will probably have given you instructions for dealing with shoplifting. If not, and should you see someone pocket an article or place it in a bag, suggest to them:

Salesperson: Good afternoon, sir (madam), may I fetch a basket for you? We like all the customers to put goods into a basket. Otherwise it's easy to forget some of your shopping when you go to pay.

Never assume that the person has taken something; you could be mistaken and it is not your job to apprehend shoplifters. There are experienced, trained personnel who will be able to conduct matters according to the law. You are simply helping in the preventive activity and, by a timely action on your part, you could prevent a shoplifting incident.

If you are sure that a person has placed an article in a pocket, a bag or other container, remember that an offence has not been committed until there is intention to leave without paying. Consider the following actual incidents that the author can vouch for as true:

A woman, with a store trolley full of provisions, walks towards the check-out desks with her friend and, such was the set of circumstances, walked through a check-out, out into the road and toward her car in the car park. As she neared the car she said to her friend, 'My god! I haven't paid!' She returned to the store and explained the situation to an equally embarrassed check-out girl.

A man was browsing for some considerable time in a well-known bookshop, and eventually selected four books from different sections. Suddenly realizing that he had stayed in the shop longer than intended, he walked quickly to the cash desk picking up a daily paper on the way, knowing that he was going to be late for an appointment. With the four books in his left hand, he presented the paper for payment and proceeded to walk out of the store. As he reached the exit, putting his hand on the door, he stopped, looked at the books, returned to the cash desk and said sheepishly, 'Sorry, I forgot to pay for the books.'

Such things can happen. In neither incident was stealing the intention, but an alert staff could have prevented what could have been serious shoplifting charges. Absent-minded people do odd things at times.

Your job is to prevent shoplifting charges. For such reasons you never use expressions such as 'You have taken' or 'You have stolen', nor must you feel customers' pockets or look in their bags. Let your head of department handle the questions.

Follow your store's instructions precisely; they have been framed to combat this problem. Shoplifting costs the retail trade millions of pounds a year. Do your best to stop it, and when you are unfortunate enough to meet with a shoplifting incident, behave with utter politeness and tact.

After-sales service

The greater part of service is carried out after the sale. Before- and during-sales service may be considered as customer servicing. After-sales service is usually regarded as product servicing, but it can also be customer servicing. No product is really 'sold' until the customer is using it and obtaining satisfaction from it.

After-sales service starts immediately after the customer says he or she is prepared to buy. You enquire, according to the store's agreed procedure, how the customer intends to pay; you complete the sales invoice, take the money, or arrange for credit terms or a hire-purchase agreement; fetch the box and packing for the product, or wrapping paper or bag; prepare the article for the customer to take away, or arrange for it to be delivered. All this is part of customer service.

In all stores there are rules governing the procedure for completing a sale, taking cash or preparing the credit formalities and wrapping goods. These should be carried out in the order laid down by management.

Always follow these procedures; they not only help your efficiency, but reduce the opportunity for shoplifting. If, as is normal, you have to show the customer a number of items, follow the instructions issued by management.

Everything that has been done to get a product into your store and to the ultimate user will be ineffective if it fails to provide complete satisfaction in its use. After-sales service is not only directed at the product itself, but also to its usage. Ensuring that the customer continues to get good use and satisfaction from the product builds goodwill and helps to promote repeat sales—if not to that customer, to his or her friends.

The type of product will obviously indicate the type of service necessary to keep it in sound condition. Domestic machines such as 'white goods' need to be serviced regularly. New products, especially complex products and those in the high technology area, may need more service in the early stages when they are new and strange to the user. Later on, as users become more familiar with them and more experienced in their operation, less servicing is needed. Also, subsequent product improvements often make them easier to use and keep in good order, and less frequent servicing is necessary.

The vast majority of consumer products, especially fast moving consumer goods (FMCG) do not require much service.

After-sales service not always obvious

A lot of products you will sell will not require after-sales service other than wrapping, bagging or arranging for delivery. But a number of products do require servicing. Many of these are obvious: washing machines, dish washers, television sets, hi-fi equipment, computers, word processors, photostat machines, and the like.

Others are not so obvious. Stair carpets should be moved about every nine months or so; curtains need cleaning at least yearly; raincoats need cleaning and reproofing; suits need dry-cleaning.

Maintaining contact with customers

Some stores keep a mailing list of customers who buy certain merchandise and, as one of their direct mail activities, send them regular letters inviting them to have the product serviced or cleaned. Considerable turnover can ensue from contracts for servicing products after the guarantee has lapsed. In particular, the annual cost of servicing high technology equipment such as photocopiers, computers, word processors and plotters, is at least ten per cent of the value of the equipment.

Small services you can offer

On a very much lower level, after-sales service includes such small but important things as opening the door for the customer; directing the way to the toilets or the restaurant if you have one; even giving advice on nearby cafés and restaurants. The sale has not been ended with the paying of the bill; you still can give a little more service.

If you are pleasant with your customers and give the impression that you are interested in them and not just in their purchases, you will often be asked your opinion on a topic or for information on the most minor matters. Where is the nearest post office? Where can I cash a cheque? Is there somewhere where I can get a key cut? Is there a shoe repairer handy? Which bus do I get for the university? The questions are endless.

You should never become upset when these questions always seem to be directed to you; you should be pleased because it proves that you are communicating with your customers and giving them that little extra that will ensure they will seek you out when they next wish to buy something from your store.

15
Making the Most of Your Time

Time is limited

What would you do if every day £86,400 was credited to your bank account, but at the end of each day whatever you had not used was lost? How would you spend that amount each day? Depending on your tastes and hobbies, you might find it easy initially to spend this amount every day, but gradually it would become difficult without planning your purchases.

In fact, every day you do have 86,400 items to your credit! Eighty six thousand four hundred is the number of seconds you have each day. No more, and no less! Every day you start with this number and, if you have not made use of any of them, you cannot use them tomorrow.

When you compare your selling day with that of a sales person who has to travel, often considerable distances, from customer to customer, town to town, you have a great advantage because customers come to visit you. You do not have to travel in search of them.

If you like your job and appreciate the opportunities for promotion by selling to customers, you are at a disadvantage because you can only stand, or sit, and wait. You cannot go out and drag customers into your store. You cannot do what the travelling sales person has to do: plan your day so that you can see the maximum number. You have to wait until customers visit you.

Maintaining interest

You will often find time apparently dragging when there are no customers around. Occasionally you may be asked to help with displays, to attend meetings, to have discussions with department heads and management, but it is easy to slip into bad habits and start discussing private business with your colleagues. You can become so engrossed in such conversations that a customer walks into your area and you don't notice. This is one of the more common 'crimes' committed in shops; doubtless, you know how frustrating it can be when it happens to you.

If you are serious about succeeding in your profession, you should develop an interest in your products. When you have the time, look at the manufacturers' literature. See if there are points about your products or merchandise that you didn't know. Even the most simple products change over the years.

Simple vegetables such as potatoes, onions, cabbages and tomatoes do not come from the same source throughout the year. Depending on the season, the country which supplies them will vary. If you are really interested in your products you will find out things such as: the tomato is not a vegetable but a fruit, and the banana is the only fruit that grows its seed outside of the fruit.

Learning facts such as these will help you develop a sincere interest in your products and automatically increase your value to your store, your customers and certainly to yourself.

Develop the habit of being curious about your products. Ask the more experienced people in the store about them. Gain as much information as you can about the goods you sell. Above all else, you should cultivate a knowledge about your products and your customers' needs.

The world's most successful company

The world's most successful company is said to be IBM, and, although their products are not simple but complex, a lot of them are sold through retail outlets. IBM's sales people are rated higher than almost any other. They have two main beliefs: first, that their products are the best that can be produced; second, that customer service is the powerhouse of their activities.

In terms of the so-called conventional sales techniques, the IBM sales people are poor performers. Where they score is in establishing a rapport with their customers, in understanding their needs and helping to solve their problems.

This means that they must know their products thoroughly. They spend up to 18 months or two years in formal training, none of it in sales techniques. Because their machines and equipment are high technology, they explore the customers' needs in depth and seek to understand their problems. The proposed solutions are therefore rooted in a customer's own experience and stated in the customer's own language, not that of a sales technique.

This approach to selling by one of the world's great companies reinforces the contention that knowledge of products and customers' needs is the secret of successful selling.

The time you have to spare in the store should be devoted to learning about the products you sell. The more experience you have selling to customers, the more you will learn how to determine what they really need and not merely what they say they need.

How to live on 24 hours a day

Occasionally we all waste time; we think we have been working or playing hard but we have wasted time. This is not to say that we should be doing something every moment of the day; we could not keep it up. But, we should be aware of how we spend our time, and make sure that we are usually making progress.

Promotion does not come to people who are always busy but are not very productive. If we seem to be occupied all the time but not producing very much, then we need to look at what we are doing with our time.

If, at the end of each day, you tried to write down how you had spent every hour, you would probably find that you could not account for a lot of your time. This is common to everyone because we all need to relax from time to time. Our aim is not to fill every minute with work, but to be aware of how we spend the majority of our time.

When you are working, ask yourself, 'Is what I am about to do, what I am employed for?' or, 'Would my management approve of what I am about to do?' If you cannot answer in the affirmative to either question, it is obvious that you must reconsider your proposed actions.

Knowledge is power

The fact that you are reading this book and have got this far is a compliment to you and shows that you are interested in progressing in the challenging business of selling. In your spare time at work, improve your knowledge: knowledge of your products, of fashions and trends, of competitors, of the town, of customers' characteristics. Because your store exists not only to satisfy customers, but to give employment to people, it needs to make a profit. You should understand what profit is, how it is calculated and how it is used. All this information is available; acquire it and use it. It will give you power.

A look at profit

If you buy a product for, say, £100 and sell it for £125, you have made a profit of £25. Profit is the difference between what you pay for an article and what you sell it for.

Suppose, however, you have to deliver it to the buyer and this costs you £5 for transportation. Your profit is reduced to £20.

This additional cost distinguishes gross profit (£25) from net profit (£20). Gross profit is the difference between the cost of acquiring or producing something and its selling price.

Net profit is gross profit less all the expenses additional to the cost of the product: publicity to attract customers; selling costs; servicing costs; and anything else that is needed for the customer to acquire and use the product. If you have to train a customer to use your product, that is a cost to be taken into consideration when you are computing net profit.

Some of these costs we can vary or control. For example, we can decide how much we are going to spend on advertising, on cleaning the store, on packing materials, and so on. Some costs we cannot control: we cannot change the amount to be paid in rent, or taxes.

A look at costs

All costs may be classified into three main groups:
- Fixed, or rigid, costs (irrespective of level of sales)
- Variable costs (which vary directly with sales)
- Semi-variable costs (tend to vary, but not directly, with sales).

This is not peculiar to retail selling; it applies to all business. If you were manufacturing products, you could substitute the word 'output' for sales in the above three descriptions.

For a retail store, examples of fixed costs are: rent, mortgage repayments, local taxes, water rates etc.

Examples of variable costs are: all products bought for resale.

Semi-variable costs include: staff, heating, lighting, power, repairs and maintenance, packaging materials, advertising, transportation etc.

To make life a little easier for those who have to keep the accounts of the store and calculate potential profits, certain costs are regarded as fixed, usually for a period of a year. Thus, staff salaries would be regarded as fixed; heating, lighting, repairs, cleaning etc and whatever else is possible would be considered as fixed for the year. This total can be divided into 12 equal amounts and considered as the fixed cost of running the store each month.

If the total of fixed costs for a year are £360,000, this could be regarded as a monthly fixed cost of £30,000. This means that a profit of £30,000 a month must be made just to pay for the fixed costs.

Speed of sales

If we are selling one kind of product, we could add to its cost a certain percentage to establish the price at which we are prepared to sell it. Thus, if we had to pay, say, £10 each, we could add 50 per cent and sell it for £15.

If we are selling many different kinds of products, we cannot add the same percentage to them all; we have to estimate the likely quantities we will sell and vary the percentage.

To products that sell very quickly — fresh vegetables, fish, some groceries — we can add a small percentage. If you consider the value of the average stock held of such products, you can see that it is 'sold' over and over again. A greengrocer may hold an average stock of fresh vegetables of, say £500. If the weekly sales are £1,000, the average stock is 'sold' twice a week. In a year, with total sales of £52,000, the stock-turn would be 100.

To products that stay in stock a long time — furniture, jewellery, watches etc — we need to add a larger percentage to pay for the costs of holding stocks that longer time. Such a store might hold an average stock of £26,000 and have annual sales of £52,000: a stock-turn of two.

MAKING THE MOST OF YOUR TIME

Percentage on cost and on return

The percentage added to fresh vegetables, groceries, and other fast moving consumer goods (FMCG) is very small. The percentage added to slow moving products is much higher. Over a year, the 'profit' achieved is similar. Thus you could have two per cent fifty times a year, or 100 per cent once a year: in each case the yield is the same.

It is easy to be confused with percentages. If you are making, say, two per cent profit and then double this to four per cent, you could say that you have increased profit by 100 per cent! First you were making two per cent, then you doubled this with another two per cent. However, the same argument would apply if you were making 30 per cent profit. If you double your profit to 60 per cent, you have increased profit by 100 per cent. When anyone tells you that they have increased their profits—even doubled them—their achievement can sound impressive, but the real facts can be hidden. Always relate percentages to actual figures: a one per cent profit is very small, but not when it is one per cent of a million!

In the example given previously, a product bought for £100 was sold for £125 making a gross profit of £25. Is this a profit of 25 per cent?

You received £125, of which £25 is profit. Therefore your percentage profit is £25/£125 = 20 per cent profit. Profit is calculated on the selling price, not on the purchase price.

Supposing you want to make 25 per cent profit: what percentage do you have to add to the cost? Let's call this desired profit 'profit on return' (POR), and the amount we have to add on to the cost 'percentage on cost' (POC). The percentage to add to cost to achieve the desired profit on return is given by the formula:

$$\text{POC} = \frac{\text{POR}}{100 - \text{POR}}$$

Therefore, to obtain 25 per cent profit, we add 25/(100 − 25) which is 25/75, or 33⅓ per cent.

If we wish to make 20 per cent profit, we add 20/(100 − 20), which is 20/80, or 25 per cent.

Gross margin and gross profit

These two terms are often used to mean the same thing but they are different. Gross margin refers to the percentage; gross profit is the actual amount of profit. Gross margin can remain the same, but gross profit will vary depending on prices and sales turnover.

In the above example, a product was bought for £100 and sold for £125. The gross margin is 20 per cent, the gross profit is £25. But if you bought a product for £10 and also worked on a gross margin of 20 per cent, you would sell it for £12.50. Your gross margin is the same, 20 per cent, but the gross profit in the second example is only £2.50.

If you operate on a gross margin of, say, 50 per cent and have a sales turnover of £100,000, your gross profit is £50,000. From this you deduct expenses to arrive at net profit. If these expenses are £40,000, your net profit is £10,000:

	£
Sales	100,000
Gross margin 50 per cent	50,000
Less expenses	40,000
Net profit	10,000

If your turnover is only £80,000, the same gross margin produces a gross profit of £40,000. Because the expenses are also £40,000 there is no net profit:

	£
Sales	80,000
Gross margin 50 per cent	40,000
Less expenses	40,000
Net profit	—

Gross margin is the same; gross profit is different. It is £10,000 less which, in this example, gives a net profit of zero.

Impact of stock

When determining gross profit, the cost of the goods sold is deducted from the sales revenue. But if the value of the stock is omitted from the calculations, a false profit is achieved. Consider, first of all:

MAKING THE MOST OF YOUR TIME

Table 15.1 Faulty Calculation of Gross Profit

	£
Sales for the year ended 31st December	450,000
Cost of goods sold	378,000
Gross profit	£72,000

A store will start and end its financial year with certain amounts of stock, verified by physical stocktaking. The opening and closing valuation of stock must be included in the calculation of profit.

Table 15.2 Correct Calculation of Gross Profit

	£	£
Sales for the year ended 31 December		450,000
Opening stock at 1 January	50,000	
Purchases for the year	378,000	
	428,000	
Less closing stock at 31 December	60,000	
Cost of goods sold		368,000
Gross profit		£82,000

The value of stock held has increased by £10,000 from £50,000 to £60,000 and this has affected the gross profit by £10,000 — from £72,000 to £82,000. Consider the effect on gross profit if the stocks had been reduced, and closing stock had fallen to a valuation of £40,000:

Table 15.3 Gross Profit with Lower Closing Stock

	£	£
Sales for the year ended 31 December		450,000
Opening stock at 1 January	50,000	
Purchases for the year	378,000	
	428,000	
Less closing stock at 31 December	40,000	
Cost of goods sold		388,000
Gross profit		£62,000

With a closing stock lower than opening stock, gross profit is also lower. The effect of having a closing stock higher than opening stock is to increase gross profit. If stock valuation had increased from £50,000 to £70,000, the result is:

Table 15.4 Gross Profit with Higher Closing Stock

	£	£
Sales for the year ended 31 December		450,000
Opening stock at 1 January	50,000	
Purchases for the year	378,000	
	428,000	
Less closing stock at 31 December	70,000	
Cost of goods sold		358,000
Gross profit		£92,000

MAKING THE MOST OF YOUR TIME

Don't imagine that all you have to do to increase your store's profits is to allow stocks to increase! But if more expensive products have been purchased during the year and not sold, you can appreciate how the higher closing stock valuation affects profit. From gross profit, all expenses are deducted to arrive at net profit, but, if stock value increases, it not only affects gross and net profit, it ties up money.

The greater the amount of stock carried, the more money that is tied up. This reduces the working capital (to give it the correct term) available for the store's operations. When working capital is seriously reduced, the company is said to have liquidity problems. We explore the problems of getting results in more detail in Chapter 19.

Learn how to handle people

No doubt you will want to earn promotion. In addition to using your time to learn about products and how they achieve profits, you should also try to understand people. You will meet a lot of people in your work. Every day you will meet different people. Yet, you will find that they tend to fall into recognizable types. Mostly, they will be pleasant, polite, easy to talk with; they will understand your explanations, and make decisions quickly. Some you will find difficult; they cannot make up their minds; they do not seem to know what they want; they change their minds and generally make life interesting and different, if not difficult, for you. You will gradually learn how to handle these people by always being patient, polite, helpful and unhurried.

You also have to learn how to live with your colleagues. They will be subject to the same difficulties, pressures, awkward customers and personal problems as you. For the person in charge of a group of people, knowing how to work with them and handle them is vitally important. The supervisor is not in charge of a group of soldiers who can be commanded to do this and do that. Although it is often said that business is a war, staff cannot be treated as soldiers. Too much pressure or 'being bossed about' and they will rebel, complain, go on strike, or give notice to quit and work elsewhere.

We hear a lot about industrial relations and human relations. What these mean is the varying inter-relationships between people over periods of time and under varying circumstances.

Although most people are reasonable most of the time, occasionally they act in an unreasonable manner. When people are in groups, they can sometimes adopt a different, often aggressive, emotion of the group.

Emotions can often be quickly fired, and are easily upset. They are rather like the beam of millions of particles aimed at an atom; sometimes one extremely tiny particle hits the nucleus and causes a violent explosion. So it is with human relationships. Occasionally, a very small and apparently insignificant incident creates an atomic explosion in a person's emotions.

If we are to learn how to get on with people and how to handle them, especially when we are in charge of their activities, we need to develop our knowledge of human relations and learn how to cope with other people's emotions.

First steps in getting promotion

The first step in gaining promotion is in devoting some of your own time to understanding what is required of a person who is made a supervisor. First and foremost, perhaps, is the quality of being able to 'get on with people'. When management is discussing the comparative merits of people being considered for promotion to supervisory and management positions, they inevitably discuss, 'how does he/she get on with the others?'

Getting on with others depends about 90 per cent on one's own behaviour. Here are eight points for you to develop:

- Be self-confident; it inspires confidence in others and creates respect.
- Be enthusiastic; as we have already said, this really is infectious.
- Learn how to be tactful in everything you say and do; this will develop courtesy.
- Learn to listen; the other person has a point of view, too, and you may find that it is better than yours.
- Make the other person feel important.
- Keep an open mind about things; do not be guided by prejudice or influenced by bias.
- Don't be afraid to praise people even though it is for something largely accomplished through your own efforts.

- Never talk ill about anyone 'behind their back'. Assume that there is always a reason for their actions or attitude.

Case Study: Betty Cook's Promotion

As Betty Cook walked into the office of Mr Percy, the personnel manager of the store in which she worked, she wondered why she had been sent for.

Her sales turnover had been increasing over the last six months. She thought that she had been very helpful to customers. She had certainly carried out all the instructions and requests made by her department head. Even the buyer had asked her opinion on four or five occasions in the last month. As soon as she walked into Mr Percy's office she realized that there was nothing wrong.

'Come in, Betty,' said Percy kindly. 'Take a seat here. I'd like to have a chat with you. Nothing wrong of course. Quite the opposite.'

Betty and Mr Percy sat in easy chairs in front of a small table.

'Cigarette?'

'No, thank you,' said Betty emphatically, 'I don't.'

'Sensible girl, too,' beamed Percy, 'neither do I. Not a nice habit and harmful to the health, isn't it? We'll have some tea in a minute. Perhaps you would like a cup. I expect you're wondering what this is all about, eh?'

'Well, I am a bit worried,' replied Betty.

'Don't feel like that at all,' he assured her. 'We've been having a re-think about one or two departments and we feel that you are ready to be promoted to another position. That is, of course, if you want it.'

Before Betty could comment, in came Percy's secretary with a tray of tea and biscuits.

'Ah! Tea!' he said. 'You take milk, sugar?'

'Please, just a little milk, no sugar.'

'Well,' continued Percy, 'we want to give Mrs Peacock more time to develop her department and we consider that she really ought to be sent on a training course. The assistant manager, Miss Meredith, is leaving soon to get married.'

'I didn't know that,' interjected Betty, surprised.

'No! It's all rather sudden. She didn't either!' mused Mr Percy, 'Her fiancé is moving abroad to join his father's company in a rather important position. They've decided to bring the wedding forward by about a year. Therefore, she's leaving shortly. Now, we would like you to accept this appointment of department assistant manager. What do you say? There would be a fairly encouraging increase in salary, of course.'

'I don't know what to say,' stuttered Betty. 'I know so little about managing. I never thought – well, I mean – if, um – well, what will

170 RETAIL SELLING

happen when Mrs Peacock goes on the course? How long will she be away? When does she go? Would I be . . .'

'Just a minute,' laughed Percy, 'I'll deal with all those questions shortly. You won't be left high and dry. But, the point is, would you like the job? Assistant manager of the haberdashery department?'

Assume that you are in Betty's position and you intend to say 'yes' to this proposition. What will be the things you will have to know and do? If there are five assistants in the department, all junior to you, what steps would you take when the announcement of your post is made known to ensure that you have their cooperation?

16
How to Improve Continually

Customers are vital to our business

When people walk into our store we are never entirely sure whether they intend to buy or are just looking. People who come in just to browse may have no intention of buying but, because of the circumstances, ambience, change of mood, opportunity, in-store display, or whatever, they become customers. Your task will often be to convert lookers into customers. Do this subtly; your appearance and manner should blend with the general atmosphere of the store and its merchandise. Assume that all who come to look around will sooner or later be customers. The following four principles stress the importance of the work you are doing:

- A customer is the most important person in our business.
- Customers do us favours by calling to see us; we are not doing them favours by serving them.
- Customers are not an interruption of our work; they are the purpose of it.
- In this competitive age, customers do not depend on us; we depend on them.

It is unquestionably inconvenient to arrive at the store first thing in the morning after a hectic journey, only to find customers impatiently waiting to be served. It is often difficult, especially after a long and tiring day in the store, to welcome yet another customer who arrives a few minutes before closing time.

The only way to overcome these feelings is always to expect customers to appear at awkward times or when you are least prepared: you will not often be disappointed.

This philosophy is similar to the good advice I received from my father when I was learning to drive: 'Whenever you drive round a blind bend,' he told me, 'always expect something to be coming the other way.' To this day, I still drive round blind bends expecting to see another car coming from the opposite direction. I am always surprised when the road is clear. But my attitude to the likely situation helps me to maintain control of what I am doing. I expect it to happen and am never caught out when it does.

You too should be surprised when a customer does *not* appear at an awkward time, or when there are no last-minute rushes before you close for the day.

Humour can sometimes improve, or relieve, a situation. I remember one day I was rushing to Charing Cross station in London to catch a train to Kent. I was late; there would be a long wait for the next train. I ran breathlessly into the station, frantically looked for the right platform, decided which one looked right and reached the ticket inspector at the gate. Panting, I gasped, 'Is this train all right for Ashford?' He beamed at me, took my ticket in a calm manner and replied in a beautifully modulated, deep voice, 'One of our very best sir: one of our very best!'

Increase in self-service

In the UK, in general, we no longer bargain over prices. In most stores, the customer is left to look around, inspect, pick up literature, and generally 'shop'. Frequently, no effort is made to sell to a prospective customer who is left alone to decide when he or she requires help or advice. It is this general attitude that has contributed to the often lackadaisical way of treating visitors when they walk into a shop.

How often, when you have walked into a strange store and looked around for assistance, have you received none? Often it is difficult to distinguish between a sales assistant and another customer. If you ask for help, sometimes you're told, 'I don't work here, I'm trying to get served myself!'

Always observe people entering your shop and decide if they look as though they might need help or whether you need to wait and watch unobtrusively for the right moment. Not everyone who walks in wishes to buy something; if your merchandise is displayed adequately and attractively, people will naturally wish to walk around and have a look.

HOW TO IMPROVE CONTINUALLY

Look efficient — be efficient

Remember that you are on show and every prospective customer who enters will mentally appraise you. If you give a poor impression, or create an unfavourable response, you are handicapped before you start. If your company does not supply you with a standard form of dress, dress attractively and without flamboyance; pay particular attention to cleanliness; shower every morning; look after your hands — they will frequently be seen close up by your customers. If you handle money, your hands will get grubby.

Without experience, it is difficult to stand around giving the impression that you are ready to help someone. If you smile continuously you will look as though you have a permanent leer. On the other hand, don't become a pouncer and pounce on everyone who walks into your area. A word of greeting or acknowledgement will establish a favourable atmosphere.

Customers come first

If you are talking to another member of staff when a prospective customer enters the store, stop talking and pay attention to the visitor. If you are talking to a superior, interrupt the conversation, saying 'Excuse me, may I attend to this customer.'

First impressions can be misleading. Be careful not to draw the wrong conclusions about customers.

Salesman:	Good morning, sir. (He addresses an untidy looking customer who has just walked into the soft-furnishing department. The customer's shoes are dirty, trousers and shirt are worn and not very clean.)
Customer:	Mornin'. I'm looking for some bedspreads.
Salesman:	Yes, sir. Single or double beds?
Customer:	Both.
Salesman:	Right, sir. Let me show you what we have.
Customer:	You sell carpets as well?
Salesman:	We do, sir, in one of our other departments. We have one of the largest selections in the area. I shall be pleased to show you. Ah! Here is a single bed with a heavy all-wool cover.

	And here is the same cover but on a double bed. May I ask what's the main colour scheme in the bedroom, sir, and would it be that your wife has a preference for any colour? (Constructing question with care in case the man has no wife)
Customer:	Not for my wife. For my daughter. I know she wants some bedspreads or covers. Thought I'd just buy them—select the colour myself. They can change 'em if they're not happy, I s'pose?
Salesman:	Certainly, sir. No problem.
Customer:	Want the carpet for the wife. If I tell you the number of beds for the daughter, and the size of the sitting room in my house, you can sort it out, can't you?
Salesman:	Yes, I can, but I'd like just a little more information about the room to hold the carpet. What kind do you have there at the moment?

The customer ordered several single and double bedspreads and a carpet, paying for the lot from a large roll of the highest denomination notes.

Don't judge by appearances

What we should learn from this transaction (which was overheard by the author in a busy country town) is that we must never make assumptions about customers from their appearance. Appearances can be deceptive. Nevertheless, in general, customers who are well-dressed and well-spoken usually buy quality articles. Such people tend to buy high quality when they can afford it. Remember also that good taste and a desire for high quality is not in itself a qualification for acquiring it. Such customers often have to buy something less valuable than they would wish.

Your task is to try to distinguish between the different types of customers so that you will be able to offer a selection of goods you think the customer would like to see.

Improving marketing knowledge

All successful retailing companies have planned their operations to satisfy the needs of a defined target market. That is, they have developed a trading policy aimed at the kind of people they want as their customers. One well-known chain of department stores has a policy of being 'never knowingly undersold'. In effect, this means that the merchandise they offer is not obtainable elsewhere at a lower price. If a customer who has bought something can prove that the same goods could be purchased from another shop at a lower price, they will refund the difference.

A chain of pharmaceuticals and toiletries stores has specialized in these fields, and developed a large range of their own brand of toiletries and medicinal preparations, all keenly priced. From time to time, they have special offers, such as three packs for the price of two, and so on.

A well-known chain of stores that sells very good quality men's and women's clothes now has an attractive food department in each store. They have a no-quibble, money-back guarantee for their clothes. And, doubtless, such is their reputation for quality and service that if you were dissatisfied with one of their food products, you could obtain a refund.

One interesting sales idea introduced by this company has overcome a problem often experienced by men buying a suit: the jacket fitted but the trousers needed to be shortened and the suit could not be worn straight away. The store recognized that two men with identical chest measurements could be considerably different in height. The sales idea was to allow customers to buy matching jackets and trousers in different sizes to get a correctly fitting suit.

The marketing mix

Marketing is concerned with finding out what goods customers need and at what prices, and promoting those goods sufficiently to sell them at a profit. It is more than just selling. Selling, as its name implies, is concerned with selling the products. Marketing not only includes the selling of goods, but the research into what products are more likely to sell, and what types, ranges, colours, sizes, etc are most popular. It determines to which segment of the market the products are likely to appeal, and estimates sales at various price levels.

For a store to become marketing-oriented, it must change the basis of its operations. Instead of simply selling what it buys, it must buy what it has calculated it can sell to customers at a profit.

When we are marketing successfully, we are satisfying customers' needs, thereby making profit. There are several good reasons why we should concern ourselves with marketing rather than with just selling.

- We need to have a thorough understanding of it so that we can do it.
- We have to give orders to our subordinates.
- We need to communicate with people in superior positions in our organization.
- We often issue instructions to people outside of our company.

When we decide to operate a retail outlet, we need to answer the following questions:

- What sort of products shall we stock?
- What general price levels shall we adopt?
- To what class and type of customers should we appeal?
- How shall we promote and sell the products?

This follows very closely the basic scheme for the development of a marketing mix. A marketing mix is concerned with five main activities:

- Product
- Price
- Place
- Promotion
- Service

Marketing obviously has something to do with the company as a supplier and the customer as a buyer; the link is the product. Companies are marketing because they supply *products* (or services) to customers.

Products are sold to make profit; therefore *price* is important.

It is no use offering products for sale where there are no people. Trying to sell most things other than, perhaps, water in the middle of an uninhabited desert would be fruitless. We must distribute the products efficiently to a *market-place*.

If you have something to sell, then you had better let potential customers know. If you don't tell, you won't sell! *Promotion* is an important aspect of marketing.

Maintaining products in first-class working condition is becoming more and more important as high technology spreads.

Adequate *service* is therefore crucial, because customers buy products to use. Customers often need to be serviced before they buy anything; this includes such things as measuring rooms, preparing estimates, quotations, surveys, proposals, etc.

You can construct a marketing plan by referring to these five words: product, price, place, promotion, service—otherwise known as the 4Ps+S.

Product

You may be selling consumer or industrial products in your retail outlet. How different customers regard your products is important for your trading policy. Apart from air, which is generally free, we all have basic needs: food, water, perhaps soap, shelter, clothes and so on.

A 'want' is less vital than a 'need', but this is purely subjective to the people concerned and, apart from essential needs to stay alive and healthy, the importance of a product will vary. Different people regard the same product as giving different degrees of satisfaction. One person will regard a TV set as a need; another will place it well down the list of priorities. Duvets for the winter may be an absolute priority for one woman; another will consider them a luxury. A portable electric saw may be regarded as an essential tool by one customer, but only as a 'want', or even 'desire', by another.

The goods in your store will appeal differently to different customers. Some things are at the top of their lists: these they regard as needs. Other products, lower down the list, are wants, or desires. Products which are classified as desires by a customer will not be bought until many other needs and wants have been satisfied.

While there can be no objective classification of needs, wants and desires, nevertheless the way customers categorize products will influence the way in which we construct plans to sell them.

Price

You have two main choices with price: to adopt a high price policy, or a low price policy. We all know of stores in certain locations in large cities which have the reputation of high quality, high priced merchandise. This is their deliberate policy of selling high class products. Other stores adopt a low price policy and advertise them strongly. This is not to say that they sell low quality goods: they have a policy of buying in bulk and selling cheap. One well-known high street grocery chain in the UK used to follow the policy of its founder, 'Pile 'em high; sell 'em cheap'. The company has long since changed its policy, but for years the original image continued to be strong in the minds of consumers.

Place

These are the channels selected by manufacturers through which they distribute their products. There are three main ways in which products can reach the actual users:

- Direct from the manufacturer to the user.
- From manufacturer to retailer to user.
- Manufacturer to wholesaler, to retailer, to user.

The size of a retailer's purchases determines whether products are bought directly from the manufacturer or from a wholesaler. Over the past couple of decades, distribution has changed rapidly. The number of small general stores, large department stores and general wholesalers has declined. Supermarkets, cash-and-carry wholesalers, mail order and do-it-yourself shops have increased in number and importance.

Promotion

Promotion covers every way in which information about products and services for sale is made known. It includes personal selling, advertising in newspapers and journals, commercial television, radio, cinema, posters, outdoor advertising, demonstrations, exhibitions and postal publicity. Most retail promotion consists of advertising in newspapers, demonstrations, window and floor displays, and sales literature.

Advertising in newspapers and sales literature requires the store to spend actual money; demonstrations are often mounted and paid for by manufacturers; displays take up valuable floor space and may, along with window displays, require trained people to prepare them.

Service

In its broadest marketing sense, service includes all those activities before, during, and after the sale that make the handling of products for your store profitable and help the ultimate user to obtain the greatest satisfaction from the product.

Some of the products in your store may require a degree of service before a sale can be completed. If you sell carpets, for example, doubtless there is someone on your staff who can visit a customer's home, take appropriate measurements, show a range of carpet samples, estimate costs, and generally discuss qualities and design.

Customers who are interested in purchasing perfume, after-shave lotion and similar toiletries like to test from a small tester bottle before deciding. If you sell clothes, you probably offer an alteration service for a nominal charge. You may have changing rooms where customers can try on things for size, fit and general appearance before buying. One well-known high street multiple has no changing facilities but has a policy of exchanging goods or returning the money if satisfaction is not obtained. This particular store has a huge exchange business at certain times of the year, especially just after Christmas when thousands of gifts are returned to be exchanged for a different size or colour.

Four main forms of service

There are four main forms of after-sales service: education, installation, routine maintenance and repair.

We need little or no education to use the vast majority of goods, but most domestic equipment, industrial machines and electronic gadgetry require some instruction. Manufacturers provide instructions on use but these vary in quality. In general, the larger manufacturers provide a comprehensive instruction book that is the size of a small manual. A leading camera, for example, has a pocket-sized instruction book in one language that is over 100 pages long. A video recorder currently widely on sale has an A4 sized manual in ten languages; it needs much concentration and practice to follow the instructions, to say nothing of operating the machine.

It is not easy to write instruction manuals. Even the most simple operations need to be thought through carefully before putting them in writing. To prove this, try writing instructions for the tying of shoe laces, or the setting up of a deck-chair.

If you sell equipment that has instructions for its use or for fitting its various pieces together, you can be of great service to the customer in explaining the instructions. Many customers, eager to use the equipment, skip through the instructions and often miss important points. Obviously, this requires that you understand the instructions thoroughly, and have practised with the actual equipment.

Service and store image

Some equipment and machines require installation. After the sale has been made, take care to organize the installation properly. I know of a case that occurred while writing this book. A customer had purchased a new, expensive washing machine and completed the transaction at the store—including arrangements for delivery and installation. The sales assistant arranged on an internal phone for delivery and ordered an instruction book in English (the one accompanying the machine was in German).

The machine was delivered on the day agreed but it was not possible to use it; the new connections on the machine did not match the old taps in the house. The customer visited a local store and tried to purchase adaptors to connect the machine, but this was unsuccessful and water sprayed out from the inadequate connections. In despair, the customer phoned the service department of the supplying store. It was then discovered that delivery and installation of the machine had not been passed on to the appropriate department, despite the fact that it was usual for equipment to be installed and delivered on the same day. They made a special call the next day and properly installed the machine.

At the time of writing, the instruction book has not been received despite a number of phone calls!

You will appreciate why this particular store does not have a very well-satisfied customer: the service provided does not match the excellence of the machine.

Routine maintenance

Unfortunately many customers think that when they purchase a new machine or piece of equipment, it will give many years' service without anything being done to it. They should be encouraged to accept that routine maintenance is necessary to keep their equipment and machines in the same operating condition as when new. Professional and industrial users are well aware of the need for regular maintenance, but this is not so with ordinary customers. If your store has a scheme, point out the benefits to the customer. If no arrangement or agreement is made at the time of buying, a note should be made to follow this up after a suitable period of time. If routine maintenance is carried out, repairs will be at a minimum because the parts that wear or deteriorate will automatically be replaced during the maintenance.

Trading policy

When preparing a store's trading policy, it is useful to develop a marketing mix. Decide what you want: what type of products, in what price brackets, with what weight and manner of supporting promotion, and with what type and degree of service. Not all parts of this mix will receive the same emphasis, of course; whatever aspect of the mix is stressed will shape the character of the store, which in turn will be reflected in its general marketing policy.

One store may aim always to stock the best quality products. It will reflect this aim in its displays, promotions and decision to opt for full-service shops, which may even include their own finance facilities. Another may concentrate on good, average quality products offered at very low prices on a self-service basis. Your store may place heavy emphasis on advertising, with weekly announcements in the local press, or monthly whole page offers promoting certain lines.

Depending on which part of the mix—product, price, promotion, or service—the emphasis is placed, the store's image will vary. If a store emphasizes the price element, it will be known for its high or low price image. If a store emphasizes the product, it will have a reputation for high or low quality merchandise (this again depends where the emphasis has been directed). Of course, you can't change the emphasis overnight. If a store wishes to change its image, this can take a very long time and may even require a 'facelift' in the form of a new shop front or even a new name.

If you understand how a store's marketing policy can be developed, you are a long way along the road to improving yourself in retail selling.

17
Buying Motives

Our real needs

In Chapters 7 and 16, we looked briefly at needs, wants and desires. In this chapter we consider them in more detail as the reasons that lie behind customers' motives for buying.

As you have seen, needs, wants and desires are not the same things. We may say that we want something, but actually need something else. A woman in a department store asks for a nightdress for her small child. What she really needs is a non-flammable nightdress for the infant. A man asks for the new style, pointed-toe shoes. What he really needs is a pair of well-fitting shoes but his desire for extreme fashion may overcome the real need.

Should you sell a customer an article which is more expensive than the price she or he has requested? This is not really a fair question, because you should sell what the customer needs and not necessarily what is said is wanted. This could mean that you have to sell the customer a more expensive article; it could equally well mean that you should sell a less expensive article.

Hierarchy of needs

Desires can be looked upon almost as expressions of hope. At the very least, they are purchases that can be put off for the time being. On the other hand, there are people who will satisfy their desires at the expense of needs. Consider people who buy cigarettes when they really need food. You could argue that smoking is a need because it is a drug and smokers are addicts, but smoking is not essential for life: it is not a true marketing need.

When you are serving a customer, try to find out what is in that customer's mind. Try to establish what the customer really needs.

BUYING MOTIVES

In a country town a middle-aged woman in an old tweed suit is inspecting a display of curtain materials. She speaks to the sales assistant.

Customer: I want some new curtaining material for my sitting room, please.
Salesman: Certainly, madam. Have you any particular colour in mind?
Customer: Well, the ones I have now are a plum-coloured velvet. I'd like a change but I'm not sure about colours. There's quite a bit of red in the carpet and it's a Turkish design.
Salesman: Is it a large room, madam?
Customer: Not really. About 30 odd by 25, I think.
Salesman: (Not listening properly about the dimensions only the words 'not really') What you need then, I think, is a fairly small design, perhaps something like this? (Shows some contemporary prints) This a Belgian weave, very nice and quite modern.
Customer: It's a little continental, isn't it? Belgian? Will the colours run?
Salesman: Certainly not, madam, especially this soft red brown. The blues and purples would be a little more difficult.
Customer: I'm not too sure about this design. My house is quite old. This is too modern.
Salesman: You would find these fit in with new or old surroundings. You may think they're modern but really they're more contemporary.
Customer: Do you have anything similar to the plum-coloured ones I have now?
Salesman: But, madam, if you want to make a change surely something to brighten up the room like this might be quite appealing. Would it help if I asked our Mr Harris to call and measure up and he can bring a range of samples?
Customer: Oh! I don't want anyone to call. I think I would like... (Picks up sample of inexpensive velvetine in an attractive plum colour) How much is this material?
Salesman: I don't think you'd really like that, madam. It's a cheap material and intended for...

184 RETAIL SELLING

Selling on the wrong motive

The woman has already walked away. The sales assistant started well but tried to sell on the wrong motive. He didn't even try to find out the real motive. All that he could establish was the colour that the woman had in mind. He also had a fixed idea of what is 'not really' a large room, but the size of the room the woman thought was not large was indeed quite large and would certainly not be found in the ordinary house.

The design in a large room generally needs to be larger than that in a small room. With the introduction of Belgian fabrics so early in the sales presentation, the salesman did not make a great deal of headway. Exactly what the salesman had in mind when he confused 'modern' with 'contemporary' we don't know!

His use of the word 'old' was not helpful. It is possible that the woman really needed the very low priced curtain material but the assistant did not explore this. He made a judgement. It is no part of the assistant's job to tell her it would not do! In effect, he was trying to sell too quickly and did not find out what the customer really needed.

Reasons for buying

Prospects who visit your store and buy, do so for various reasons. If your store has a self-selection or self-service layout, you will not often have the opportunity of selling to customers. However, when you do, you should try to find out the customers' reasons for buying.

One well-known refrigerator company, when training the household goods sales staff of the stores where their refrigerators are on sale, teaches the use of two opening questions to be put to customers who stop and look at their models:

Salesperson: Good morning (afternoon), madam. Is this the type of refrigerator you have at home?

The customer can answer in a number of ways but it is unusual to receive the reply 'no' or 'yes': there is usually an explanation. Here are some examples of the replies the sales people receive:

No, we have a very old one.
No, the one we have is smaller but different.
It's not as modern as this one; what's the top for?

BUYING MOTIVES

We've one very similar, but it's much older.
We don't have one.
No, this is much slimmer; I see the door is used for storage too.
Yes, but I'm looking for another.
No, we thought it about time to get a new one.
Yes, exactly. We bought one last month. It's excellent.

From the reply to the first question, the salesperson will know whether or not the customer is a prospective buyer because there may be an indication of a possible need. A reply such as the last one requires a special response, which is dealt with separately. With each of the other replies the salesperson proceeeds to the second question:

Salesperson: May I ask how many you cater for at home?

Once again, the replies are wide but supply additional information:

Just my husband and me.
There's just four of us.
Oh, only myself and my husband (wife).
I live on my own.
Six in all; my husband and four children.
Depends. My son works away a lot of the time.
It varies, but usually about five.

The second reply, coupled with the first one, indicates whether the customer may be in the market and, if so, what size would be best. Where the customer has already purchased one, the salesperson can simply ask whether they are thinking of buying another, perhaps as a gift.

Practically every home has a refrigerator so people are familiar with their operation. The main market is for newly-weds and people who are intending to replace the one they already have.

Both types of prospective customer will be interested in any new features which are available, although of course each customer will favour a different feature. Some models have a separate deep freeze compartment, some have internal lights, some automatically defrost themselves. For some customers, the ease of buying on credit or hire purchase means that price is often not as important as the 'down payment'. What is important to you is figuring out the customer's individual reason for buying—finding the buying motive, in short.

Select motive on which to sell

Some people rate the preservation of food and 'left overs' very high; others are more interested in the use of a fridge as a cooking aid. Others like to have lots of cold drinks. With carefully phrased questions, you can determine what line to take with your sales presentation. If the customer expresses a keen interest in the preparation of elaborate cold desserts, you would not start to discuss the economies that could be made by using a freezer compartment to store large quantities of food bought on sale.

Similarly, if the customer said that too much food was being wasted because the present fridge was not working properly, you would be missing a selling opportunity if you started to talk about the automatic defrosting mechanism.

Find out the buying motive of the customer and then link it with the benefits of the product.

It is a mistake to try to sell a product on price if the customer wishes to buy on quality. Equally, it is a mistake to sell on quality if the customer has a certain amount in mind to spend.

There can be no selling without buying. Strictly speaking, you do not sell anything to anyone: *you create the conditions in which the customer buys.*

Where the sale takes place

Thus, a sale takes place in the mind of the buyer. We repeat, because it is so important, that every remark you make, every word, every gesture, must be made with the aim of making the right impression on the buyer's mind.

It is not easy to understand human behaviour and determine reasons why people behave as they do. Every customer you meet is different and reacts in a different way to the same stimulus. Their backgrounds are different, their values are different. Such basic differences are usually permanent aspects of personality and influence everything that is done. Habit becomes merged with personality. This background of habits and personality is a person's 'frame of reference'. Our particular frame of reference influences everything we do and how we think about things. It makes us conservative or radical; optimistic or pessimistic; happy or miserable; cautious or adventurous, and so on.

Observe and listen

You can learn something about customers' frames of reference by observing their dress, jewellery, watch, rings and accessories and the particular items they carry. Remember, however, that we are not trying to determine whether or not a customer has the money to purchase a product. We are considering his or her general background in an attempt to establish what kind of motives will induce that prospective customer to buy.

Even more illuminating than observing customers is talking with them. By listening to their speech and its quality and content, you will be able to make a more accurate estimate of their frame of reference.

You will decide that some people need to be sold on quality; others on value; some on status, economy, pride of possession or fashion. By assessing a customer's general background, that is, their particular frame of reference, you are guided as to the best way to develop your sales presentation.

Susceptibility of customers

The same person can be entirely different under different conditions. A customer who is pleasant and easy to talk with may be intolerant in a hot, stuffy atmosphere. A woman who has had a poor night's sleep will be an irritable woman in the morning. A man who has just returned from his annual holiday will still have the memories of his vacation in mind. These may be pleasant or otherwise, but whatever they are, they will influence his present feelings and behaviour. The clerk who has just won a sizeable sum of money in a competition is a different person from the clerk of last week. The woman who has just been promoted is a different woman from yesterday.

Making the right impression

If you intend to make the right impression on customers, you must consider their possible buying motives carefully.

This is difficult when you are in an open-plan store and do not actually sell to customers; even in a full-service shop it is difficult because customers often do not know the reasons why they buy some products. They tend to rationalize their purchases and mostly buy from habit or because they are convinced of the uniqueness of some particular product.

You may have seen the television commercial for a washing powder where a housewife in a supermarket is holding her weekly purchase of a new powder. The interviewer offers her two packets of her old powder for the new packet she has selected. So strong is her conviction of the washing effectiveness of the new powder, that she refuses the two-for-one offer.

I know of a housewife who lives in Luxembourg and travels to France to purchase a brand of washing powder not sold under that name in Luxembourg. Although it would be possible to buy an identically formulated powder with a different brand within a hundred metres or so of her home, she is convinced that the French powder is better.

There is no real difference between brands of similar categories of powders; the distinction lies in their advertising claims and the strength of their publicity. But the difference created in buyers' minds is very stong. Product differentiation is not necessarily in the product but a measured distinction in buyers' minds.

After we have purchased basic necessities, our scale of preference varies for products that are not essential. If you think about your most recent non-essential purchase you may find it difficult to remember the actual buying motive that made you acquire it!

Find out the real reason

You will remember that there are at least two reasons why we do anything—a good reason and the real reason. A young woman may express an interest in buying a new skirt and discuss various reasons why she wishes to purchase it. The real reason may be that one of her friends has recently bought a skirt and she does not wish to feel less than equal. She would never admit this, but if you made a remark such as, 'That suits you very well. You'll create some envy with your friends,' this could close the sale. It could make just the right impression; you would have tapped the true buying motive that she couldn't or wouldn't disclose. Of course, she might not even be aware of her real motive!

Urge to buy a new product

A man is considering the purchase of a new car. He may be buying a particular model to enhance his status but he is unlikely to give this as a reason. He will talk about fuel consumption, safety, durability, running costs, comfort, performance, and other matters. The real reason for buying the particular model is never discussed.

How many men would admit that there is very little wrong with their present watch, pen, radio, typewriter or hi-fi set, except that it is becoming an embarrassment to their ego?

How many women would admit that the real reason for buying new curtains is because friends are coming to stay?

Frequently, when people are on holiday, they visit the local shops and buy something new: a pair of shoes, a pair of trousers, a hat, a shirt, skirt, blouse, gloves, record, book, bracelet.

It is not wrong to want to buy something new. In fact, if we only ever bought a product when the old one was no longer usable, there would very soon be an enormous depression in the economy. The reason for buying is not often to meet a need, but to answer a want or desire.

Rationalizing the buying motive

You cannot ask customers for their real motives for buying, but you can listen to their conversations. Sometimes their accents will indicate that they are not local people, but are on holiday. Ask questions; while there are often complicated motives for buying, there are also fairly simple ones near to the surface. Others can be rational motives clearly expressed by the customer; your sales presentation can then easily make points that will link with these motives. Once the customer is able to rationalize the purchase with acceptable reasons, the sale can move quickly to the close.

Customer: Do you have a winter coat in that new shade of brown?

This might indicate that the customer is fashion-conscious because she has indicated that she knows the 'new' shade.

Customer: I'm looking for a really warm coat—preferably in the new shade of brown.

This customer may be trying to reconcile two buying motives, functional and fashion. You cannot be sure of her real buying motives and therefore you must ask questions—explore a little further and listen carefully.

Suppose you decided that the customer is more concerned with a warm coat than with the new shade, what would you do? Here are some questions that you should not use; they are poorly constructed.

- What price do you have in mind?
- Are you looking for a fairly good coat or would a relatively inexpensive one do?

They have not been well thought out and, although the words 'relatively inexpensive' are better than 'cheap', the innuendo is still there. What you are trying to establish with this particular customer is whether she wants a high or low-priced coat, and how important the new shade is to her. You cannot go straight to these points until you have explored a bit more. At this point you might say:

- Are you interested in a particular style?
- Is there something you have seen that you like?
- For town wear, madam?
- Full length, madam?
- Is there a particular model you have in mind, madam?

Don't rush your sales presentation; help the customer to buy. Try to decide by listening attentively to the customer's statements and questions whether there is a fairly clear motive for buying or whether you have to seek it. If you rush into your presentation without establishing some of the customer's basic needs or wants, you might suggest points that are irrelevant.

A useful selling technique is to repeat a point made by a customer in your presentation and to link it with a product benefit.

Customer:	I want a really warm coat.
Saleswoman:	Is there a particular model you're interested in, madam?
Customer:	No. I'm just looking.
Saleswoman:	Have you seen the new winter range from XYZ with the mylar lining?
Customer:	No.

| Saleswoman: | I'll just fetch one for you. (Returns with coat) Here you are, madam. I think this is your size; don't worry about the shade for the moment. If you're looking for a really warm coat for the winter, this is really something. |

The saleswoman has decided that this customer wants little technical information about the coat and will be receptive to ordinary day-to-day language. This is why she used the words, 'this is really something.' Of course, she will be able to explain how the reflective lining was originally developed for use in space suits, and to give the customer as much data as required.

Price as a motive

Do not consider price as a buying motive unless a customer says: 'I want such-and-such a product and wish to pay up to X; will you show me something not more than that, please?'

You might suspect that, even in this example, price is not the buying motive. You are right; people do not buy things because the price is low. You wouldn't buy a tube of toothpaste because it was only a few pence. You wouldn't buy bargain priced shirts that had been wrongly cut and had very short tails that would ride up over the trousers. You wouldn't necessarily buy any particular item simply because the price is low. If you don't have a fireplace in your home, what is the value of a cheap coal scuttle?

Why we buy products

No one buys a product for itself but for the satisfaction it gives. If the customer insists on knowing the prices of the various models you show, the real motive is not price but value. Price is only part of the proposition; the other part is quality. The two together make up value. Never attempt to sell a product on its price. Sell it on its value—even if it's at a give-away price!

18
Advertising

Advertising media

Advertising is a tough, professional business. It is very easy to spend money on it. To advertise simply means to make known; it does not mean to make sales. Remember the discussion of the marketing mix in Chapter 16. There are five aspects to the marketing mix: product, price, place, promotion and service.

To make sales, you must have the right products that customers will buy; they must be on offer at prices that customers are prepared to pay; they must be in stock and available when customers call. You must have sufficient staff to serve customers when they call and to deal with their enquiries and questions when they are buying; you must have adequate maintenance and repair facilities to service the products they purchase from you.

This covers the product, price, place and service: the fifth component of the marketing mix is promotion.

My first job was delivering newspapers morning and evening. Four times a day, I would see a small, decorated wooden notice that was hanging behind the newsagent's counter. It had an illustration of two men; one looking down a well, the other climbing a palm tree. It had the rhyme:

> The man who whispers down a well
> About the goods he has to sell
> Will never make as many dollars
> As he who climb a tree and hollers!

You might have the finest products available at the very lowest of prices, but if you don't tell anyone, you won't sell them. The reason that advertising alone does not mean sales is because you must have a product; moreover, the product must be available when the customer wants it, at a price he or she will pay.

It is for this reason that sales are not necessarily in proportion to the amount of advertising. If you increase the amount spent on advertising by, say, ten per cent, it does not follow that sales will increase by the same, or even a related, percentage.

Advertising is delivering messages to people by means of a medium. This medium can take a number of forms—hence the use of its plural, media. There are five main media: newspapers, journals; commercial television; outdoor and transportation posters and signs; radio; cinema. In the UK, throughout the 1980s, average advertising expenditure has been fairly steady:

Press	65%
Television	28%
Outdoor advertising	4%
Radio	2%
Cinema	1%

Apart from these main five media, there are exhibitions, postal publicity, printed literature, sales contests, demonstrations, and many more.

Retail store advertising

Before an advertising campaign can be planned, you must have a marketing plan which defines the types and ranges of goods, the classes of customers sought, and in which areas, and the product prices. With this information you can prepare advertising suggestions. The primary task is to transmit information about the merchandise to the prospective market. This is a communications activity: transmission and receipt of information. It is important to understand this two-way flow. No one can communicate alone; it takes at least two people—one to transmit and one to receive.

When preparing advertising it is helpful to have a reasonable idea of the target audience—in other words, of those people who are likely to be interested in the store's range of products. The emphasis should not be on the attributes of the merchandise but on what customers are actually buying.

Study competitive offers from other stores. It is unlikely that you have merchandise unique to your store and therefore any sales that you generate will be taking away business from stores in the area. This means that you must offer a better deal, a better service, a better store. Look at your competitors' ads in the local papers. You may conjecture that they are advertising what is selling; but don't assume that what they are doing is right, and don't copy their style.

Stress what is important

Stress what is important to prospective customers and not what is obvious about the products. If it is easy to see that the product is a pretty party frock for children, concentrate on the party spirit and the enjoyment that little girls will receive. If it is easy to see that the product is small, don't say so in the ad, but stress the benefits of compactness. Do not waste advertising money stressing obvious product attributes; describe some of the benefits that are not so obvious.

If you advertise a line of products, make sure you have sufficient stock for display in the windows and the store and for sale. If a line is very limited, question the wisdom of spending money advertising it. Your advertising must be complementary to the marketing plan. Don't dissipate your promotional efforts. Don't advertise one product in the local press, have a window display of different products or make it hard for customers to find the advertised product in the store. Concentrate your total promotion.

Maintain your image

Maintain a general, main image of the store in all your advertising and promotion. This starts with the use of the same name and same style of lettering. If your store has its own name style, use it in advertising, on the delivery vans, on the letter heading, price tickets, store cards and so on.

Beware of all who suggest a change of image by 'going up market', changing the range of merchandise, altering the style of name or introducing a large range of low priced products. There are many stories of stores, even well-known ones, who have made this elementary but serious error. Attempting to change the image of a retail store is costly and can only be achieved over a long period when the changes are not radical or violent and are not readily noticed by the current customers.

Offer a promise

Offer a definite promise in your advertising copy by stressing the satisfaction that customers will obtain from the products. It has been estimated by an American advertising executive that over $1000 million have been spent promoting products using these six words: cool, new, power, relief, refreshing and white.

Do not rely on verbal messages for advertising. Put your creative strategy in writing and circulate it to everyone connected with sales. Then, when you consider advertising suggestions, ask yourself: is it compatible with the store's creative strategy?

Make your advertising objectives reasonable and attainable. The first is relatively easy; the second will depend on the quality of the advertisements and whether potential customers see them.

Importance of the medium

Getting your message over to the target market is more important than creating brilliant advertising that wins awards for design. This does not mean that you can have mediocre adverts; it means that you use the right media to transmit your messages.

To illustrate with an obvious example: supposing your store has purchased a special line of copper-bottomed aluminium saucepans for use on electric cookers. It would be of no use obtaining a list of gas customers and sending them a direct mail shot advertising your saucepans. No matter how brilliant the illustrations and explanatory text, no matter how much of a bargain they are, no one who cooks with gas is going to buy pans meant for use on an electric cooker.

There is often a tendency for professional advertising people to pay a lot of attention to the actual advertisement, to its layout and artistic impact. This is important; but more important is getting the message to the right people. The medium really is more important than the message.

Of course, the quality of your advertising must reflect the general image of your store. If you have a store piled high with low priced merchandise, you can have advertising that is 'busy' and hard selling. If your store is well laid out with well-designed displays of your more important products, then your advertisements must be well-laid out and present an image of order and organization.

Appropriate media

Apart from the large west end stores in London and other major cities, stores will normally draw their custom from a local catchment area. The size of this area will depend on the size, attraction and comprehensive nature of stock held by the store, the population, the density of population, the nearness of the store to a major centre with large shops, local competitive stores, the public transport system and the availability of a store car park.

The appropriate media to reach the people in the catchment area will be the local newspapers, local outdoor poster sites, and printed leaflets. If the catchment area is large, local radio and commercial television may be suitable.

If there is a high degree of specialization, it would be appropriate to use national papers for mail order purchase.

A large, central store in London can consider its catchment area as the whole country, and use national papers and wide commercial television coverage.

Newspaper advertising

The proposed ad should be photostated and pasted in a recent copy of the newspaper. If the ad is to appear on its own, and not with other ads, paste the photostat on a page containing editorial matter.

Close the paper, and then skip through it. Does your proposed ad impress you? Is it bold and does its message come across quickly? Don't read it but continue skipping through the paper and determine what is transmitted to you in that brief glance at your ad. This will give you a general idea. Now look at it analytically.

The headline and name of the store should project the essence of the ad. Whatever you are announcing in the ad should come across in the headline and be linked with the store. Only about 20 per cent of readers get beyond the headline. If you are depending on an explanation below the headline to get your message across, you are wasting 80 per cent of your advertising money.

You will have decided on the target market. The headline should appeal to that market. If you are advertising to housewives, single them out in the headline by a direct or indirect appeal: 'Make him happy tonight', 'Tempt him with these new ideas', '(Store's name) has the answer to your house cares.'

News about new products, new ideas, new ways of doing things, new stock, new shoes, anything new, is powerful in a headline and will be read. If you have actual news, punch it out in the headline: 'New, turbo-charged lawnmower cuts cutting time in half!'

Be positive. Ads with a negative approach, such as those that used to advertise a brand of aspirin and list dozen of aches and pains it would relieve, are not read. Where appropriate, use the words already mentioned that attract attention: cool, new, power, relief, refreshing, white. Direct the reader's attention to the positive benefits of your merchandise.

If you use an illustration, use one that will reproduce well in the newspaper and will not look muddy. In general, photographs are better than drawings although, with certain products, notably motor cars, it is sometimes better to commission a drawing with the important or salient features enhanced.

For many years, a well-known London menswear store used an artist who accentuated the height of the men in the ads, shortened their arms and gave a bronzed look to their skin. The effect, though anatomically inaccurate, was impressive. The tall, elegant men always had the appearance of having just returned from some far-off overseas appointment, and were ready for any eventuality.

If you are advertising a particular product that improves something, use 'before' and 'after' photographs. And if you have a person in the 'after' illustration, she or he should be beaming with pleasure.

Two main advertising situations

There are two main types of advertising situation: where ads are looking for readers; where readers are looking for ads. The latter generally occurs in specialist publications: do-it-yourself magazines, cars, stamp collecting, shooting, fishing, and so on. Readers of magazines in these categories usually buy the thickest one—the one with the most adverts. The former is the more usual situation with newspapers and general magazines—the ads are attempting to gain the attention of the readers who are primarily interested in the editorial matter.

Because newspaper ads are not actively looked for by readers, you have to attract them to your particular advertisement. If it is with others on a page, it will have to contain some pretty strong attraction to be read. If it exists on its own with only the paper's editorial to keep it company, it will receive a higher degree of attention. However, these solus ads (their technical name) are more costly than ordinary, ROP ads (run of paper), which are inserted where convenient to the paper.

If your store has an image to maintain, it is better to have your ad 'trade set' by a professional typesetting house; you then supply the newspaper with the complete ad in the form it requires. If you instruct the paper to set your advertisement (this is called 'paper set'), you will probably be disappointed with the result because it may not possess the typeface your designer has specified and the paper's compositor will use the nearest face.

Sales literature

This section also applies to store catalogues and brochures. After personal selling, printed sales literature is the most important method of getting your sales messages over to prospective customers. It is therefore worthwhile making sure that you obtain the best possible product.

Do not use a representative of the printer for the design; use a professional designer. The objective of the literature should be agreed. The designer is given a draft copy and illustrations and a thorough briefing on what the literature is to be used for, how it will be distributed, the type of people who will receive it, what it is hoped to achieve, and the constraints such as the store's name style, colour scheme, and budget. The object of this briefing is to ensure that little alteration has to be made at a later stage.

The copy will be written in a style appropriate to the store. The designer will also: mask the illustrations for printing; obtain other photographs if necessary; write the captions; and finally, prepare a mock-up. The mock-up should be circulated to the appropriate people in the store and, unless there are any strong reasons for change, it should then be sent to the printer for printing. Alterations at the printing stage are costly.

Production of adverts and leaflets

The arrangement of illustration and descriptive text is called the 'layout'. The illustration may be a photograph or drawing; the descriptive text is usually referred to as the 'copy'.

ADVERTISING 199

First, a few rough sketches are prepared, known as 'roughs'. The copy is written and an indication of typeface to be used is given. Machinery, electric motors, and industrial products will have a strong, sometimes bold, typeface. For fabrics, women's clothes etc, a delicate face is best; for professional products, computers, office machines, a clean, modern face is generally preferred. For the bargain offer, the typeface must create the impression of speed; perhaps a rough, hurried, or half-finished typeface. Look at well-known stores' advertising to gain an idea of the typefaces for various products.

With all ads and sales literature, the copy must fit the space yet be set in a large enough typeface to be read easily.

Printer's measure

The printer's system of measurement originated in the early days of printing when printers were mainly occupied with book production for the church. Type varies in width according to the size of the letter; 'i' and 'l' are each about a quarter of the width of an 'm' and a 'w'. This gives proportional spacing, whereas an ordinary (non-proportional spacing) typewriter gives the same number of letters in the same width of line.

It was, and is, not possible to describe the length of a line by stating the number of type used in its formation; it depended what letters the line contained. In effect, each line of type contains a varying number of letters.

However, as the height of type is the same for all letters, that is, the blocks of metal containing the letters are the same height—only the widths vary—height became the basis of printer's measure.

The first book to be printed regularly was the Pica, a 15th century book of rules about church feasts. The typeface with which this was mostly printed had six lines to the inch; its size became standard and known as pica size type. The inch was divided into 72 points, and thus pica type (six lines to the inch) is 12 point size. All other faces were described in terms of points.

24 point type is a third of an inch high; 6 point typeface gives 12 lines to the inch; 10 point, just over seven lines to the inch. Type is usually set with horizontal spaces between the lines. These spaces are called 'leads' and may be any size from one point upwards. Leaded lines are easier to read than if the matter is set 'solid'; but it increases the area occupied by the text.

How many words?

Will the copy for the ad or leaflet fit the available space? What space is needed for a given number of words?

First, consider the size of the typeface. It is no use setting an ad in very small type; for example, 6 point (12 lines to the inch) would not be read. You need at least double this—12 point.

You can gain an impression of various type sizes by measuring the number of lines per inch of printed matter. If you count six lines to the inch, it could be 12 point type, but it is likely to be leaded and have a 1 or 2 point lead between the lines, and would therefore be 11 point set on 12, or 10 on 12. Books are mostly set in 11 point on 12 (11 point type with 1 point leading).

To complicate life, we have a mixture of imperial and metric measures. We measure length and width in metric and compare the space with the point system. Table 18.1 gives the approximate number of words of an average typeface in various type sizes that will occupy 10 cm^2 (ten square centimetres). When using this table you must make allowances for typefaces, especially some of the modern ones, which are wider than the average.

Table 18.1

Type size	*Words per 10 cm^2*
6 point solid	73
6 " leaded	53
8 point solid	50
8 " leaded	36
10 point solid	33
10 " leaded	25
11 point solid	26
11 " leaded	22
12 point solid	22
12 " leaded	17
14 point solid	17
14 " leaded	14
18 point solid	11

Suppose you have a space 15 cms long and 12 cms wide. This is 180 cm^2, or 18 units of 10 cm^2. For 12 point leaded, the table indicates that this space would take 18×17 = 306 words approximately. If you wanted 14 point leaded, the calculation is 18×14 = 252 words.

If half the space is to be an illustration, you can have approximately 150 words in 12 point, or 125 in 14 point, both leaded.

Outdoor advertising

The outdoor media your store is most likely to find of value include posters, small billboards, and possibly panels on transportation. Many stores also display posters on their own premises.

The same principles apply to all types of posters. Use sites near the store or near where your target population lives. If you are advertising products, show them as large as possible and in full colour. Because people only have a very short time to look at a poster, crystallize the main product benefit in a short message; about six words is ideal.

People should be able to identify your store as soon as they see the poster. If they have to travel within a few metres of it before recognizing it, the poster is not bold enough. If you have to approve a poster suggestion, don't look at it while holding it in your hand; have someone place it upright several metres away and then glance at it.

Emotion, especially humour, works with posters, but it must be almost instantly understood, otherwise it will be wasted. On occasion, some national advertisers use 'clever' posters and the viewing public has several months to work out their meaning. It is only because these advertisers have a large appropriation and a great amount of more direct advertising that they can afford to experiment in this way.

19
Getting Results

The losing product

Sooner or later you will be promoted and become more responsible for profitable results. The more you know about budgeting and profit planning, the better for your future. Each store has its own procedure for its annual planning and budgeting, but the following general principles apply to all stores.

To make the principles clear, the figures have been kept fairly simple. However, the same principles apply irrespective of the complexity of the accounts.

A store sells four main products: A, B, C, and D. The profit for the previous year was £12,250 on a turnover of £450,000. However, product B is giving cause for concern because it lost £4000. Here is the breakdown:

Table 19.1 Revenue Account for Four Products of XYZ Store for 19X4

	PRODUCTS				
	A (£)	B (£)	C (£)	D (£)	Total (£)
Sales	100,000	50,000	175,000	125,000	450,000
Cost of goods	81,600	40,500	143,400	102,500	368,000
Gross profit	18,400	9,500	31,600	22,500	82,000

(continued overleaf)

Table 19.1 continued

	PRODUCTS				
	A (£)	B (£)	C (£)	D (£)	Total (£)
Selling expenses	9,000	7,250	12,000	10,000	38,250
Advertising	1,000	1,000	1,500	1,000	4,500
General overheads	2,750	2,500	3,200	2,800	11,250
Administration	1,600	1,500	2,000	1,650	6,750
Other expenses	2,250	1,250	3,000	2,500	9,000
Total costs	16,600	13,500	21,700	17,950	69,750
Profit	1,800	(4,000)	9,900	4,550	12,250

What would you do about this? Would you recommend that the product is dropped from the range? It appears obvious that if it were dropped, profit would be increased.

This problem is not as straightforward as it looks, and requires an understanding of costs. All costs have two parts: a fixed part and a variable part. The fixed part includes rent, rates, insurance, probably staff salaries and wages, advertising and anything else that the financial people are confident will remain relatively fixed for the period, usually a year. The variable part varies with sales. If you supply bags with products, the higher the sales of products, the greater the total cost for bags because they vary directly with sales.

If you dropped product B, the variable costs associated with it would not be incurred. But the above account does not show the variable costs. The costs of selling, advertising, general expenses, administration and sundries are simply deducted as overheads.

Overheads

An 'overhead' is an accounting term. It is those costs that cannot be traced to a particular product. The lighting, heating and general maintenance in your store would be difficult to allocate to products. Just imagine calculating how many different individual products have been sold in a year and then dividing all the overheads by that number. The cost of doing it would be prohibitive. How would you allocate the cost of, say, training! Would you assume that all products carry an equal proportion of the training cost? Would you include all products, or all products sold?

A lot of costs are not allocated to products because it is inconvenient, impracticable or too costly to extract them and to relate them to individual products. They are lumped together and called an overhead.

With the above accounts, the first thing we ask for is an analysis of the sales, advertising, general, administration and other expenses. We find the following:

- Selling expenses include salaries, wages, travelling.
- Advertising expenses are for press advertising and literature.
- General expenses are rates, lighting, heating, repairs, depreciation.
- Administration expenses are professional charges, post, telephone, etc.
- Other expenses are long-term loans and overdraft interest.

Further investigation indicates that it is not practical to allocate any of the general, administration and other expenses to products; they are best left as a fixed overhead. The new information enables the following account to be prepared.

Table 19.2 Calculation of Contribution for 19X4

	PRODUCTS				
	A (£)	B (£)	C (£)	D (£)	Total (£)
Sales	100,000	50,000	175,000	125,000	450,000
Cost of goods	81,600	40,500	143,400	102,500	368,000
Variable sales exes	5,500	3,000	6,150	8,100	22,750
Variable advg exes	950	500	1,500	800	3,750
Total cost	88,050	44,000	151,050	111,400	394,500

(continued overleaf)

Table 19.2 continued

	PRODUCTS				
	A (£)	B (£)	C (£)	D (£)	Total (£)
Contribution	11,950	6,000	23,950	13,600	55,500
Fixed overheads:					
Selling				15,500	
Advertising				750	
General overheads				11,250	
Administration				6,750	
Other expenses				9,000	
Total fixed overheads					43,250
					£12,250

Contribution

Contribution means contribution by a product to the total of fixed overheads and profit. The allocation of costs to products continues until it is impracticable to go further; all the remaining costs are collected and shown as fixed. In this account, the total of fixed overhead is £43,250.

This is a much better presentation of accounts for management decisions. You can see the following contributions:

	(£)	(%)
Product A	11,950	22
Product B	6,000	11
Product C	23,950	43
Product D	13,600	24
Total	55,500	100

206 RETAIL SELLING

Product C is producing nearly half of the total contribution and product B only just over 10 per cent. Supposing you decided to drop product B. Here is the contribution table 19.2 with product B dropped:

Table 19.3 Contributions with Product B Dropped

	PRODUCTS				
	A (£)	B (£)	C (£)	D (£)	Total (£)
Sales	100,000		175,000	125,000	400,000
Cost of goods	81,600		143,400	102,500	327,500
Variable sales exes	5,500		6,150	8,100	19,750
Variable advg exes	950		1,500	800	3,250
Total costs	88,050		151,050	111,400	350,500
Contribution	11,950		23,950	13,600	49,500
Fixed overheads:					
Selling				15,500	
Advertising				750	
General overheads				11,250	
Administration				6,750	
Other expenses				9,000	
Total fixed overheads					43,250
					£6,250

Profit has dropped from £12,250 to £6,250! Dropping what was thought to be a losing product would cost the store £6,000.

This is the exact amount of contribution of product B—£6,000: if we drop it, we lose its contribution.

This form of presenting accounts enables management to compare products more easily because all the costs and expenses that can be applied to that product have been; the result is the net contribution to overheads and profit.

Previous years

When budgeting and generally projecting figures for a new year, it is useful to see what has happened in the most recent years. The last four years' trading figures of this store are given in Table 19.4.

Table 19.4 XYZ Store Revenue Accounts for 4 Years

	19X1 (£)	19X2 (£)	19X3 (£)	19X4 (£)
Sales	331,600	372,600	414,000	450,000
Cost of goods	265,280	294,350	331,200	368,000
Gross profit	66,320	78,250	82,800	82,000
Expenses:				
Selling	26,860	31,300	33,950	38,250
Advertising	3,500	4,000	4,500	4,500
General	8,950	9,690	9,500	11,250
Administration	5,300	5,400	5,750	6,750
Other	7,290	7,820	7,850	9,000
Total costs	51,900	58,210	61,550	69,750
Net profit	14,420	20,040	21,250	12,250

The accounts have been further analysed and the product contributions for the previous three years set out in 19.5, 19.6, and 19.7.

Table 19.5 Calculation of Contribution for 19X1

	A (£)	B (£)	C (£)	D (£)	Total (£)
Sales	72,950	53,050	112,740	92,860	331,600
Cost of goods	58,390	42,450	90,190	74,250	265,280
Variable sales exes	3,510	2,300	8,400	5,800	20,010
Variable advg exes	750	390	1,200	660	3,000
Total cost	62,650	45,140	99,790	80,710	288,290

Table 19.5 continued

	A (£)	B (£)	C (£)	D (£)	Total (£)
Contribution	10,300	7,910	12,950	12,150	43,310
Fixed overheads:					
Selling				6,850	
Advertising				500	
General overheads				8,950	
Administration				5,300	
Other expenses				7,290	
Total fixed overheads					28,890
					£14,420

Table 19.6 Calculation of Contribution for 19X2

	A (£)	B (£)	C (£)	D (£)	Total (£)
Sales	81,980	55,890	130,410	104,320	372,600
Cost of goods	61,430	44,700	105,620	82,600	294,350
Variable sales exes	4,400	2,680	10,740	6,590	24,410
Variable advg exes	830	420	1,200	750	3,200
Total cost	66,660	47,800	117,560	89,940	321,960
Contribution	15,320	8,090	12,850	14,380	50,640
Fixed overheads:					
Selling				6,890	
Advertising				800	
General overheads				9,690	
Administration				5,400	
Other expenses				7,820	
Total fixed overheads					30,600
					£20,040

Table 19.7 Calculation of Contribution for 19X3

	A (£)	B (£)	C (£)	D (£)	Total (£)
Sales	91,080	62,100	144,900	115,920	414,000
Cost of goods	72,860	50,300	115,200	92,840	331,200
Variable sales exes	4,750	2,650	11,500	7,500	26,400
Variable advg exes	770	400	1,240	690	3,100
Total cost	78,380	53,350	127,940	101,030	360,700
Contribution	12,700	8,750	16,960	14,890	53,300

Fixed overheads:	
Selling	7,550
Advertising	1,400
General overheads	9,500
Administration	5,750
Other expenses	7,850
Total fixed overheads	32,050
	£21,250

Comparing the years

There are a number of ways in which these figures for the four years could be analysed and compared, but the most significant table is 19.4. This shows the net profit figure falling from a high of £20,040 in the second year to £12,250 in the most recent year. Obviously, much more work would be necessary before decisions on actions could be taken. Here are three tables comparing the contributions of products in money terms (19.8); in percentage of total sales (19.9); and as percentages of the year's total contribution (19.10).

It has been mentioned before that percentages can often conceal a serious situation; which of these tables gives you a more realistic picture?

Table 19.8 Four Years' Contributions

	A (£)	B (£)	C (£)	D (£)	Total (£)
19X1	10,300	7,910	12,950	12,150	43,310
19X2	15,320	8,090	12,850	14,380	50,640
19X3	12,700	8,750	16,960	14,890	53,300
19X4	11,950	6,000	23,950	13,600	55,500

Table 19.9 Contribution as Percentage of Year's Product Sales

	A (%)	B (%)	C (%)	D (%)	Total (%)
19X1	14.1	14.9	11.5	13.1	13.1
19X2	18.7	14.5	9.9	13.8	13.6
19X3	13.9	14.1	11.7	12.8	12.9
19X4	12.0	12.0	13.7	10.9	12.3

Table 19.10 Contributions as Percentage of Year's Total Contribution

	A (%)	B (%)	C (%)	D (%)	Total (%)
19X1	24	18	30	28	100
19X2	30	16	26	28	100
19X3	24	16	32	28	100
19X4	22	11	43	24	100

Use of money costs money

If your store is making eight per cent profit a year and borrows money, or operates with an overdraft, which costs, say, ten per cent a year, it is losing money. Because stores operate on low profit margins, it is important that they control the flow of cash. If they have to borrow money to fund too large a part of their operations, they become unprofitable.

Most shops sell for cash. If credit is required by the customers, someone has to pay the interest on the amount of money outstanding. If the rate of interest is, say, 12 per cent, that is, one per cent a month, every £1000 outstanding costs £10 each month in interest.

Small shopkeepers with limited funds prefer to invest in stock and not in funding credit to customers. If too much credit is given, the shopkeeper has insufficient funds to buy new stock.

No matter how large the store, the use of money costs money. If a large London store decides to refurbish a department at a cost of £500,000, this amount of money is not then available for investing in goods. Until sufficient profit has been made to pay for the refurbishing, either the current rate of interest will have to be paid on the half million or, if it is from the store's own cash reserves, the store does not have the use of that money. It could have been invested and earning money. Either way, the store has to pay for the use of the money.

Cash flow

Cash flow is the difference between cash being received and cash being paid out. If the cash coming in is greater than that going out, cash flow is positive. If cash is going out faster than it is coming in, cash flow is negative.

Here is a simplified example of a shopkeeper with an annual turnover of approximately £250,000. Sales are about £5,000 a week and no credit is given to customers; the cost of goods sold is about 80 per cent of price. Purchases are made for cash, to obtain a small discount, every four weeks in line with sales.

Table 19.11 Cash Flow

	WEEKS					
	1 (£)	2 (£)	3 (£)	4 (£)	5 (£)	6 (£)
Sales	5,000	4,500	4,800	5,200	5,000	4,800
Purchases	10,000				16,000	
Wages	500	500	600	600	500	500
Overheads	450	450	450	450	450	450
Cash out	10,950	950	1,050	1,050	16,950	950
Cash in	5,000	4,500	4,800	5,200	5,000	4,800
+ or (−)	(5,950)	3,550	3,750	4,150	(11,950)	3,850
Balance	(5,950)	(2,400)	1,350	5,500	(6,450)	(2,600)

Negative balances are shown in brackets. There is a negative balance four weeks out of the six. Interest has not been shown in this simplified example but you can see the need for careful control of cash. Sales for the first four weeks totalled £19,500. If the shopkeeper wishes to keep his stock at about the same level he needs to buy a similar amount which, at the average of 80 per cent cost, is £15,600. As you can see, £16,000 was actually spent.

By understanding the importance of costing, budgeting, profit planning and cash flow, you will improve your chances of promotion.

20
Interpersonal Relationships

Human interactions

In retail selling, as with many similar jobs, you are constantly interacting with other people. We often hear, 'This job would be all right if it were not for the students, the passengers, my colleagues, the customers...'! Sales people complain that some customers are very difficult to get on with. We all become frustrated in our interpersonal relationships at times.

By understanding how such relationships are governed, we can improve our interpersonal communications.

The human recording machine

Some years ago, a Canadian neurosurgeon, Dr Wilder Penfield, suggested a basis for an explanation of human behaviour. The type of surgery he performed required that his patients were fully awake during the operation. While the patient's brain was exposed, he found that when he touched certain parts of it with a weak electric current, the patient re-experienced events that had apparently been long forgotten.

The patient 'relived' the events. If there were smells or sounds connected with them, the patient reported being able to smell and hear them again; any particular emotion associated with the recorded event was re-experienced. Dr Penfield concluded that the brain acted like a living tape recorder and recorded everything experienced from birth.

Dr Eric Berne used this information to develop his theory of transactional analysis. According to Dr Berne, every human being has three main parts, or three main persons, within his or her personality. These are: Parent, Adult and Child. Every day, at different times and in various circumstances, we act and talk from our Parent, our Adult or our Child. When we are being helpful, or critical, such as our parents were, we are acting from our Parent. When we are being logical, reasoning from information to decide on the best course of action, we are acting from our Adult. When we are acting or reacting in an emotional manner, excitedly, amusingly, angrily, hysterically, etc, we are acting from our Child.

Parent

Everything that has happened to us since we were born has been permanently recorded in our brain. Everything we experienced as very young children with the adults around us has been recorded and built into a store of data described as our Parent. All the constraints, the rules, the strictures, all the hundreds of 'don't do that', 'do this', 'stop that' that we heard, have been stored in our brains ready for replay in response to appropriate stimuli. Just as Dr Penfield's electric proble evoked reactions, so certain incidents and situations in our daily life can trigger reactions.

Unless we are aware of this and take a conscious action to do otherwise, these automatic responses are the same as those we heard or saw in our parents. Parental response may be critical or nurturing. When we act in a critical, moralizing, reprimanding or punitive manner, we are in our critical Parent. When we act in a caring, sympathetic, encouraging, protective manner, we are in our nurturing Parent. This is exactly as our parents acted from time to time, according to circumstances.

Adult

The part of our personality that reasons out things from the facts is the Adult. While the Parent makes automatic responses based on attitudes or 'what is right', the Adult assesses situations, compares the data with stored information and makes logical, unemotional decisions.

You can understand the difference between the Parent and Adult if you consider a situation in which you are a sales manager interviewing a man for a sales position. You decide not to employ him because of the way he expresses himself. On what basis do you make that decision? If his answers and ideas were completely at odds with yours, and you decided that he was not going to 'fit in' with your team, then you probably made your decision in the Parent. However, if he had spoken poorly and was unable to express himself adequately, and you know that clear expression is essential for successful selling of your products, then your decision was probably made in the Adult.

Child

The Parent is the taught part of our personality; the Adult is the thought part; the Child is the felt part. While we were growing up in our Parent, we were also recording our Child tapes. These were internal reactions to the growing up process, primarily feelings about ourselves and other people. The Child recordings include those very early experiences of curiosity, joy, imagination and spontaneity, and the later childhood problems of frustrations, anger, inadequacies, and helplessness.

There are a number of facets to the Child recordings. The natural Child is the one that does what it wants to do, and when. It acts with joy or anger, with fun or petulance, is often adventurous and sometimes rebellious. When we behave impulsively, do things without thinking or are aggressive or fearful, we are acting in our natural Child. Everyone possesses a natural Child but learns to adapt its behaviour to create our adapted Child. This adapted Child is understanding, complying and courteous, but may also be reactionary and rebellious when adapting to circumstances.

Yet another facet of our Child was developed from the time we learned how to manipulate our parents and others. We discovered that we could avoid unpleasant situations by our cute, attractive behaviour, or by introducing humour, comedy or distractions at the appropriate time. While this facet of the Child is intuitive, creative and even logical, it is, above all, manipulative.

We three

We are all three persons—Parent, Adult, Child—and all three are used in our everyday life. But the Adult should govern our actions and determine when to switch off the Parent and Child tapes. If you are aware of these aspects of personality, it will help you to understand how and why people behave in different situations and how they respond in a controlled manner, or react instinctively.

Normal behaviour

Normal behaviour needs to be defined. If you put your hand on something that is, unknown to you, extremely hot, you jump back and probably shout out. You react instinctively from your Child.

If you have an appointment and a friend says, 'I think it's time we were going,' and you reply, 'Yes, I'm ready. Let's go,' both your friend and you are speaking from the Adult.

If you are trying to connect two parts of a product together and you drop one on the floor, you may shout out angrily: you are acting from your Child.

If you have had a tiring morning shopping and a colleague asks, 'May I help you with that?' and you reply, 'Thanks — I'm exhausted,' your colleague is speaking from the Adult and you have replied from the Child.

If a subordinate has persistently disobeyed you, you probably become angry and remonstrate with that person. You talk from your Parent.

If a customer walks up to you in your store and says, 'good morning', and you reply 'good morning', this is normal behaviour. From Adult to Adult.

All these are examples of normal behaviour. During the course of any day, although we usually act in our Adult, we also act in our Parent and our Child as appropriate, and other people respond similarly from all three parts of the personality. Reasoning behaviour is to talk and act from the Adult to another person's Adult. As I am writing this book, I am acting from my Adult and hoping to hook your Adult. But to act in one's Adult all the time would create a monotonous situation and, from time to time, we act from our Child and introduce a little emotion or make a joke.

You may remember an earlier incident in Chapter 5 in which, during an ordinary conversation, Adult to Adult, between a customer and the salesman about a faulty connection between washing machine and the water tap, the salesman spoke from his Child and caused the customer to laugh with, 'It's only recently that you've been getting a shower with the washing?'

We need to introduce variety into our speech, talking mainly from our Adult but occasionally with a little humour, when appropriate, from our Child. It would be a very dull existence if we never laughed.

Crossed wires

Occasionally, you will talk from your Adult to a customer's Adult but, instead of the customer responding from his Adult, he responds from his Child to your Parent. Consider:

Salesman:	May I book your order? (A−A)
Customer:	I wish your company would keep you informed. I've already sent it in by post. (C−P)
Saleswoman:	May I look in here to see if I can find it? (A−A)
Colleague:	For goodness sake! I've already looked in there (C−P)
Salesman:	May I see your copy of the order? (A−A)
Customer:	How many more of you people want to see it? I've already shown it to the other chap. (C−P)

Whenever the topic or subject is abruptly diverted, rather than simply complemented, you should suspect a crossed wire, or crossed transaction. These crossed transactions have to be retrieved by you. If the other person has responded from the Child to your Parent, instead of replying from your Adult, you must complement the response and reply from your Parent to the other's Child.

In each of the above three examples, the salesperson would need to explain to the other the reason why the question was posed (that is, talk from the nurturing Parent).

By determining how our colleagues and customers react we can obtain an indication of how we are behaving. If, for example, they respond in the Adult, we are likely to be acting in our Adult. If they consistently respond in their Child, we may be spending too much time in our Parent, especially if their Child is heavily stressed. If they are heavy in their Parent, we are most likely to be in our Child too much.

Ideally, we should develop Adult to Adult relationships with the occasional Child intervening to lighten situations.

Recognizing Parent, Adult, Child

It is not always easy to recognize whether a person is acting in the Parent, Adult or Child. Also, there is often movement from one to the other in the same conversation. By listening to the words used and the tone of voice, and observing the body expressions, you will obtain clues to that person's state of mind.

Here are some words, actions and tones of voice to indicate behaviour.

Parent

Words	*Nonverbal language*	*Tone of voice*
never	scowl	critical
always	look of disapproval	sneering
do	index finger pointing	supportive
don't forget that	pat on the back	consoling
should	consoling touch	severe
careful	arm round shoulders	sympathetic
don't	holding someone	encouraging
what will they say!	furrowed brow	protective
don't worry	arms folded	
the rules	shaking head in disapproval	
yesterday	nodding head in approval	
be good		
keep quiet		
because I said so		
let me help you		
listen		
try		
don't be afraid		
you're: right, wrong, good, silly, etc.		

Adult

Words	*Nonverbal language*	*Tone of voice*
I think	faces speaker	relaxed
where	curious look	objective
what	eye to eye contact	inquiring
who	nodding in understanding	placid
when		clear

Adult *(continued)*

Words	*Nonverbal language*	*Tone of voice*
in my opinion	erect but not tense	soft
probably	attentive	
I'm interested	thoughtful	
what do you think?	alert	
my reaction would be	relaxed	
let's have a look	confident	
what should we do?		
the reason is probably		
you'll find that		

Child

Words	*Nonverbal language*	*Tone of voice*
Oh!	wide-eyed	whining
mine's better	sulking	affectionate
smashing; terrific	laughing	playful
I love it	flirty	baby talk
try and make me	swaying	joyful
get lost; push off	withdrawn	excited
exclamations: ouch, bah!, ruddy 'ell, etc	guilty look	teasing
if only	dancing	complying
was I right?	sexual	
ha! ha!		
oh yeh!		
everyone's against me		
I can't win		
I'm always being put upon		

An apparent paradox

Your job is to help customers, yet you should never ask a customer 'Can I help you?' Better to say, 'May I help you?' It is a question of grammar. The phrase 'can I' really means asking if it is possible. 'Is it possible to get to the other side of the town by using this bridge?' or, as we would normally ask, 'Can I get to the other side of town over this bridge?'

The phrase 'may I' is asking permission—perhaps permission to use the bridge. 'May I use the bridge to get to the other side?'

'Can I help you to repair your word processor?' 'No, I'm afraid you can't because you don't have the knowledge.'

It's not being pedantic; you are there to help people; if you ask if you 'can', you are stating the obvious.

How to greet customers

A better approach to prospective customers is to say 'Good morning, madam (sir), let me know if I may help you.' The use of a statement rather than a question shows that you are 'in control' of the sales proceedings. You have the knowledge of many products on sale and customers may need your assistance. They need help and guidance, but only when they have partly made up their minds.

If they have no preconception of what they want, they will want to look around and collect their thoughts and will then probably ask you for information.

Customers want information

Does the machine work off batteries? How long do the batteries last? Can they be recharged or do I have to buy new ones? How much do they cost? And how long did you say they lasted?

What is the fabric made of? Will the colours run if I put it in my washing machine? How does it differ from wool? Why is it so expensive? Why is this light one more expensive than the heavier one?

If I don't like it can I change it? Can I buy part of it today and buy the other part next week? Could you deliver it? I'm not home during the day and would need to make a special point of being there when your driver arrives. Can you arrange this?

Knowledge linked with an understanding of human behaviour is a powerful tool in retail selling.

Giving information creates confidence

The well-trained salesperson will be able to deal with these questions. If you can cope with them in a confident manner, you will create confidence with the customer. You should also develop a relaxed relationship when talking with customers; smiling when it is appropriate. You will give the impression of being completely at ease, and on top of your job.

Control the sales presentation

You are a professional sales person; therefore, when you are dealing with customers, learn to control the sales presentation. If you are going to sell, as opposed to merely taking orders and writing out bills, you need to learn how to control the sales presentation. You needn't be afraid of this. It is simply learning how to maintain control of the presentation (but not necessarily of the conversation) in a skilful manner and how to keep it directed to the customer's problems and needs.

Knowledge is the key to control

The foundation on which you build your control procedures is knowledge—knowledge of your goods and their uses: How are they made? How do they work? How are they serviced? Why do they cost what they do?

At the start of a conversation with a customer you possess the knowledge of your products; the customer has the knowledge of his or her circumstances and a certain amount of knowledge of your products and similar or competitive products.

Some of the knowledge possessed by the customer may be inaccurate. Because you are the professional, you will have the latest, up-to-date knowledge about products and you cannot expect the customer, who does not normally have the same facilities as you, to know as much as you. Unfortunately, many customers do not realize that modern technology progresses every year. New ideas, new ways of making things, inventions, new materials and improved methods all tend to make the average customer's knowledge dated.

Out-of-date knowledge

A friend of the author, when much younger, used to service his own car and became very skilled. Even now, he can listen to a faulty engine and make a reasonable estimate of where the fault is located — fuel or ignition. One day, some years after he had stopped servicing his own car, his wife asked him for help as her car would not start.

He reasoned that the problem was a weak spark at the plugs and found that one of the cables from the distributor to a spark plug had no metal wire inside. (In fact, none of the cables has metal wire inside any more; modern technology uses a different means of getting the spark to the plugs.) You can understand the gap in knowledge between the man who asked for some high tension cable and the motor accessory salesman who served him with something that he had never seen!

Objections are natural

When customers raise objections to buying a particular product, they are acting in a perfectly natural way. You must never feel upset, disappointed or annoyed that they are raised; be surprised if they aren't! We have looked at various ways of dealing with objections; the best way of course, is to prevent them from arising in the first place. But you can't know all the possible objections that might be raised, so you should always be ready to deal with new ones.

Objections are not always welcome

Sometimes it is suggested that customers who raise objections do so because they are interested in the product; otherwise they would not make objections. Taken to its logical conclusion, this argument implies that all we would have to do would be to make sure that all our customers raised objection after objection about the product, and then we would close every sale!

A customer who says, 'I'm sorry, that's much too expensive; I don't want to pay as much as that,' is raising a perfectly acceptable objection. It's no good saying that the product is worth the price; that would be replying from your Child. The customer has spoken from his or her reasoning Adult; you must repond from your Adult. You have to establish whether the objection to price is the real reason for not buying.

INTERPERSONAL RELATIONSHIPS 223

You may not have convinced the customer that the product is worth the price and this must be dealt with in a different way. What sometimes sounds like an objection is really a request for further information.

Objection? Use your Adult!

When dealing with objections, use your Adult. Listen carefully to what the customer says; understand exactly what the customer is objecting to. Do not interrupt but listen until it is obvious that the customer has finished.

When the customer has finished, re-state the objection in your own words. You have listened, understood, and replied from your Adult.

Customer: (Stating an objection to the salesman who is listening very attentively) I think I prefer the article made by a smaller company that specializes in it. This is all right but... well... y' know... a specialist makes a better product.
Salesman: (Politely, earnestly) How would you classify a company that is a specialist in the manufacture of this product?
Customer: Well, not too large, and all the employees work on this one type of product.
Salesman: Ah! The specialist company has all its employees concentrating on one general type of product.
Customer: Exactly!

The salesman has responded from his Adult, and used the barrier-erecting technique discussed in Chapter 4. He re-states the objection in slightly different words, confirming that he has understood it, and created a barrier, so preventing the customer from retreating behind it.

Know your product's benefits

Only use this technique of re-stating the objection if you have a product that will deal with it. It convinces the customer that you understand the objection, and are not arguing about it. The salesman above continues:

Salesman: (Handing customer a catalogue) May I show you this photograph in the company's catalogue? Here is their plant, which has been developed on the same site for over fifty years. They are specialists in the manufacture of this product. Every one of their three hundred-odd employees is engaged in its production.

You will not always be able to deal with an objection as dramatically as this, but always act in your Adult: listen carefully, then reply.

Be succinct

When possible, convert the objection into a question. Do not respond from your Child and raise a smokescreen of words in the face of an objection. Be precise and concise.

Customer: I like it, but it doesn't look very strong.
Salesman: (Takes hold of the plastic and tries to tear it in half) Is this strong enough, sir? I can't tear it. Would you like to try?

The objection that it is not very strong has been turned into the question as to whether it is strong enough!

Never argue with customers: that would be responding from your Child. This temptation is strongest when an untrue objection is raised.

Customer: No. I don't think I'll have this rug. Rugs like this always curl up at the edges after a while and we trip over them.
Salesman: (From his Child) That's not so with this rug, madam, if you don't mind my saying so. I can show you the manufacturer's guarantee which...
Customer: No, thank you. I'm not interested. Good day.

The salesman has started to argue with the customer. Win an argument and lose a sale. Even start to argue and you may not have the customer hanging around!

Customer: No. I don't think I'll have this rug. Rugs like this always curl up at the edges after a while and we trip over them.

Salesman: True, madam. An excellent point. Some rugs can be very dangerous. (The salesman is responding from his Adult, agreeing with the customer's objection) Do you know why this curling happens?
Customer: Well, wear, I suppose.
Salesman: The manufacturer hasn't taken care to keep the selvage even in the weaving, and there isn't sufficient body in the rug to stay flat. Feel the weight of this rug. (Offers rug) Also note the label guaranteeing even selvage. This is your guarantee of a rug that will not curl.

Make a note of the various objections you receive and how you answer them. You can then introduce these answers into your future presentations and prevent the objections from arising.

Put the objection in the sales presentation!

Supposing you were getting a number of customers questioning the apparent high price of a product. You would know the reasons for that higher-than-expected price, and you would therefore be able to deal with the objections to it.

Use those reasons in your presentation and you will be giving the customer information that justifies its price. It cannot subsequently be raised as an objection; you will have mentioned it before the customer does!

Customer: Ooh! I like that coat.
Saleswoman: Yes, very nice, madam.
Customer: How much is it?
Saleswoman: £125.
Customer: Oh! That's very expensive.
Saleswoman: (Reacting from her Child) Not really, madam. In fact, it's less than you'll find it elsewhere. But good materials like these are always more expensive and the...
Customer: Well, I'm sorry, I don't think I want it, thank you.

The saleswoman should have responded from her Adult.

Customer: What a splendid coat!

Saleswoman: I don't wonder it caught your eye, madam. The sheen makes it look like silk, but it's pure virgin wool, crease resistant, (screws the material in her hand) shower-proof, light and very warm. For the price you have top coat and raincoat. Just slip it on.

Any objection to the price has been partly pre-empted by including what was originally an objection in the sales presentation!

The best way of dealing with objections is to avoid them. The best way of preventing them from being raised is to raise them first in your presentation to a customer.

By listening carefully, acting from your Adult and trying to hook the other person's Adult, you will develop a good selling personality and maintain good interpersonal relationships with colleagues and customers.

Case Study: The Grocery Survey

You are employed by Fine Fair Ltd, a grocery chain and your managing director, Stephen Goodman, has just called you into his office. He says, 'I'd like you to have a look at the results of the survey that has been carried out by *The Grocer*. Perhaps you can let me have your views as to what changes you think we should make in our merchandising policy?'

He hands you the following survey. A total of 1750 shoppers were interviewed in the Midlands area of the UK. Most of those interviewed were women. The area was divided into convenient sections and electoral registers were used to make random selections of houses. The refusal rate was well under 0.5 per cent. The average age of women interviewed was 40, and 80 per cent of those interviewed had children.

Table 1

How often do you shop for groceries, not including the times when you have forgotten something?

	%
More than twice a week	7
Twice a week	11
Once a week	66
Every two weeks	11
Every three weeks	1
Less often	2
Miscellaneous	1
No response	1

Table 2

On what day or days of the week do you usually do most of your grocery shopping?*

	%
Monday	10
Tuesday	6
Wednesday	7
Thursday	25
Friday	42
Saturday	32
Sunday	6

* More than 100% because shopping on more than one day.

Table 3

How often do you make up a shopping list before you go shopping for your groceries? Would you say:

	%
Usually	56
Sometimes	20
Seldom	12
Never	12

Table 4

What is the main reason you do most of your grocery shopping on that day?

	%
Most convenient time; only time available	50
It's pay day; fits payday schedule	31
Good day for specials	27
Habit	14
Not crowded on that day	8
Stock up for the weekend	7
Leaves the weekend free	6
Run out of food usually on that day	6
Better selection of groceries	3
Miscellaneous	13

* More than 100% because of multiple answers.

Table 5

How far away, in terms of time, do you live from the store where you usually do most of your shopping?

	%
Less than 5 minutes	35
5 to 10 minutes	48
11 to 15 minutes	10

Table 5 (continued)

	%
16 to 20 minutes	3
21 to 25 minutes	1
26 to 30 minutes	1
Don't know and miscellaneous	2

Table 6

Approximately how long are you in the store when you are buying your groceries?

	%
Less than 20 minutes	4
20 to 40 minutes	29
41 to 60 minutes	28
Over an hour	36
Don't know, varies	3

Table 7

At which *one* store do you shop for groceries most often?

	%
Sainsbury's	12.2
Tesco	8.4
CoOp	7.9
Liptons	5.7
International	4.7
Kwick-Save	4.5
Fine Fare	4.5
Gateway	4.4
Spar	4.2
Budgen	3.2
Others	40.3

Table 8

What stores are within easy reach of you but at which you do not shop?

	%
CoOp	16.3
Tesco	16.3
Sainsbury's	13.0
International	12.3
Liptons	11.2
Gateway	7.8
Fine Fare	6.5
David Greig	6.3
Budgen	5.8
Spar	4.3
Cullens	4.3
Express Dairy	2.9
Others	42.2

Table 9

What are your reasons for shopping at (name of shop) most often?

	%
Close; nearby	40
Discounts; low prices; specials	37
Good meat	26
Carry all brands	24
Know the assistants	22
Good fresh produce	15
Clean store; stock well displayed	13
Good service; adequate parking	13
From habit; miscellaneous	47

Table 10

What are your reasons for not shopping at (name of store) regularly?

	%
Prices too high; very few special offers	45
Too far	26
Prefer the shop I go to now	24
Only go occasionally	18
Poor selection	15
Unattractive store	7
Slow check-out	7
Too small	7
Very overcrowded; too busy	5
No particular reason	3
Miscellaneous	46

Table 11

On your major grocery shopping trips, how often do you buy some advertised special offers? Would you say:

	%
Frequently	15
Occasionally	20
Seldom	25
Never	38
No response	2

Table 12

Which of the following do you consider to be your best source of grocery advertising? Which second and which third?

	Source		
	1st	2nd	3rd
Newspapers	42%	14%	15%
Store leaflets	24%	25%	15%
Door-to-door circulars	13%	22%	20%

230 RETAIL SELLING

Table 13

How often do you refer to the following three publicity media when making shopping trips? Would you say:

	Newspapers	Leaflets	Circulars
Once a week	81%	76%	57%
Once every two weeks	8%	5%	8%
Once every three weeks	1%	2%	3%
Once a month	3%	5%	8%
Less often	6%	12%	24%
No response	1%	—	—

Table 14

Please look at all these advertisements and tell me the reference number* of the one you like best.

	%
International	18
Fine Fare	18
Liptons	14
Gateway	13
Budgen	8
Tesco	8
Sainsbury's	7
CoOp	4
Cullens	1
Express Dairies	1
No response	1

* Some of the adverts did not carry the name of the store.

Table 15

Why do you like the advertisement you picked as best?

	%
Large, easy to read; large print; plain	42
Eye catching; attracts attention	38
Easy to find the individual items	27
Special offers are easy to find	19
Low prices; more bargains	17
Good assortment; variety; different products	15
All other responses none more than 8%	45
No responses	3

INTERPERSONAL RELATIONSHIPS 231

Table 16

Ads thought to be by:	Advertisements Placed By:									
	Sainsbury %	Tesco %	International %	CoOp %	Fine Fare %	Gateway %	Budgens %	Cullens %	Liptons %	Express %
Sainsbury	33	3	3	2	4	2	2	*	3	1
Tesco	5	27	3	3	3	2	2	5	5	2
International	1	1	20	1	2	2	1	7	1	1
CoOp	4	1	3	17	6	2	4	1	3	1
Fine Fare	1	2	2	*	17	3	2	*	2	1
Gateway	3	2	2	1	3	17	3	1	2	1
Budgens	*	1	1	*	2	2	8	1	2	1
Cullens	1	2	2	*	*	*	1	6	1	1
Liptons	2	1	1	5	3	1	3	*	4	1
Express	*	*	2	*	1	*	1	4	*	4
Don't know	39	45	43	53	46	53	52	61	56	66
Other	4	6	9	9	7	7	11	6	12	10
No response	7	9	9	9	6	9	10	9	10	10

* = Less than 0.5 per cent.